CCCC Studies in Writing & Rhetoric

BEFORE SHAUGHNESSY

Before Shaughnessy

Basic Writing at Yale and Harvard, 1920–1960

Kelly Ritter

Southern Illinois University Press
Carbondale

Printed in the United States of America

12 11 10 09 4 3 2 1

Publication partially funded by a subvention grant from the Conference on College Composition and Communication of the National Council of Teachers of English.

Library of Congress Cataloging-in-Publication Data
Before Shaughnessy : basic writing at Yale and Harvard, 1920–1960 / Kelly Ritter.
p. cm. — (CCCC studies in writing & rhetoric)
Includes bibliographical references and index.
ISBN-13: 978-0-8093-2924-3 (alk. paper)
ISBN-10: 0-8093-2924-7 (alk. paper)
1. English language—Rhetoric—Study and teaching (Higher)—Case studies. 2. Report writing—Study and teaching (Higher)—Case studies. 3. Academic writing—Study and teaching (Higher)—Case studies. 4. Writing centers—Case studies. I. Title.
PE1404.R523 2009
808'.042071173—dc22 2008054836

The paper used in this publication meets the minimum requirements of American National Standard for Information Sciences—Permanence of Paper for Printed Library Materials, ANSI Z39.48-1992. ∞

We often think that we define terms,
but terms also define us.

—Kathleen Blake Yancey and Brian M. Morrison,"Coming to Terms: Vocabulary as a Means of Defining First-year Composition"

CONTENTS

ACKNOWLEDGMENTS

I would like to thank the following individuals who helped me to conceptualize, revise, and complete this project: Joseph Harris, Duke University; Deborah Holdstein, Columbia College Chicago; Alfred Guy, Yale University; Nancy Sommers, Harvard University; Scott Ellis, Southern Connecticut State University; Stephanie Vanderslice, University of Central Arkansas; Diane E. Kaplan, Yale University Manuscripts and Archives; Tim Driscoll and Robin Carlaw, Harvard University Archives; Bianco Falbo, Lafayette College; and Kristi Fleckenstein, Florida State University. Finally, I thank my English department colleagues at the University of North Carolina at Greensboro for their generous ongoing support of my research.

This project also would not have been possible without a sabbatical leave award from Southern Connecticut State University for Fall 2007 and a Connecticut State University Research Grant for Summer 2007.

And, as always, I thank my husband, Joshua Rosenberg, and my daughter, Sarah Rosenberg, for their ongoing love and support.

Portions of chapters 2, 3, and 4 appeared as the article "Before Mina Shaughnessy: Basic Writing at Yale, 1920–1960" in *College Composition and Communication* 60 no. 1 (September 2008): 12–45.

BEFORE SHAUGHNESSY

Introduction: Relocating Basic Writing

THIS BOOK IS ABOUT the long history of so-called basic writing, that which began before the work of Mina Shaughnessy and the rise of open admissions and which was taught at elite institutions such as Yale and Harvard. The interrogation of this somewhat-forgotten history is important to me, because as I enter my fifteenth year of teaching first-year college writing, already I have had the opportunity to work with basic writing students at three distinctly different universities, each of which redefined "basic" in context. My first basic writing class was at my doctoral institution, the University of Illinois at Chicago (UIC), the urban branch of Illinois' flagship state university. My second class was during my time as a full-time lecturer at the Sweetland Writing Center at the University of Michigan, an elite public institution situated in the prototypical Midwestern college town of Ann Arbor. Finally, my third class was at my previous institution, Southern Connecticut State University (SCSU), a regional, comprehensive state university in New Haven, Connecticut, where I was a tenured faculty member and writing program administrator. Each of these institutions presented its own version of "basic" writing—and basic writers—and thus in the aggregate gave me a new, and ultimately paradoxical, view of this course and its inhabitants.

At UIC, my so-called "basic" writers were in a summer program designed to help at-risk students enter the university without need for preparatory course work. The course was English 150: Introduction to English Composition, and it carried three credits toward graduation. These writers were largely Latino/a men and women from Chicago; they were first-generation students who almost all lived at home, spoke Spanish with family members (but were fluent in English), and worked thirty-plus hours per week. The class enrolled fifteen students who met eight hours per week for five weeks of the summer term. What classified them as "basic" in the context of the UIC curriculum was primarily a limited sense of intellectual training—that is, a severely prescribed schooling in the virtues of the five-paragraph theme, chiefly as a result of parochial secondary-school classrooms—resulting in a limited vocabulary with which to describe, reflect upon, and analyze texts. These students were not visibly lacking "basic" skills in grammar, structure, and the like, but they were clearly lacking a larger *social and intellectual context* in which to employ a more sophisticated lexicon. As a result, they wrote clean but uninteresting and linguistically very "safe" essays; by the end of the term, they were venturing into more complex territories of language (and subject matter) as a result of our brief but intensive writing course. My UIC students were what I call Basic Writer Type #1, what many assessment rubrics would describe as "limited" or "minimally competent."

At the University of Michigan four years later, my basic writers were students in Michigan's ECB (English Composition Board) 100: Composition Practicum. The course carried two credits toward graduation and met once weekly. These students were a far more mixed bag than what I had encountered at UIC. Many were second-language learners (Korean, Russian, and Japanese, for just three examples). Some were native speakers, but all were very tentative writers and were in possession of very low self-confidence, partially due to being local, less-privileged students than their out-of-state, wealthier counterparts. All self-placed into ECB 100 via Michigan's relatively new (at the time) placement system, in which students responded to a series of questions about their reading and writing practices in order to determine in which course they would be most comfortable: ECB 100, English 125, or another writing-intensive, introductory course in the liberal arts curriculum.

My Michigan class was very small—capped at only ten students—and the pedagogy of the course dictated individual attention to each of them, with group conferences held every other week in lieu of class.

These "basic" writers were, by and large, students who were anxious about their ability to live up to the relatively lofty expectations of the Michigan curriculum where writing (or any subject) was concerned. Even the second-language writers were, in my assessment, already "prepared" for the demands of first-year writing but chose to place themselves in ECB 100 for, as one student put it, "some extra time" to develop as writers. Hence, my Michigan students were Basic Writer Type #2, what rubrics would describe as "competent" or even "highly competent" but whom instructors would describe as "hesitant" or " unpracticed in writing." At a less-competitive, less socially stratified university, I could see these students easily enrolling in the standard first-year writing course, if not Honors or accelerated English.

At SCSU, I encountered yet another version of "basic" writers. This time, my class, called English 098: Composition Writing Lab and carrying zero credit toward graduation, probably more closely resembled what most teachers, students, and the general public picture when conjuring an image of basic writing. I again had a small group—capped at twelve—this time filled with many versions of "basic" that were differing portraits of underpreparedness. As an extreme example, there was a student I will call John. John was returning to college after a long absence; he was twenty-six years old, a head chef at a restaurant in downtown New Haven, and a graduate of a vocational high school. John had tried college briefly once before and had dropped out. Motivated by his family's desire to see him graduate and his own perception that college was "the right thing to do," he had now reenrolled and was seeking a degree in—well, he didn't know exactly *what*, but he was going to give it a try.

I had worked with all sorts of writers up to that point—second language, learning disabled, native speakers from developmental to advanced, adult/nontraditional, and traditionally aged first-year college students. But nothing prepared me for John. Congenial and hard-working almost to a fault, pleasant in class and helpful with other students, John literally could not write a sentence. His error patterns fit nothing I had ever seen before. He wrote without punctuation, without paragraphs, without boundaries or markers of any kind. He usually spelled words right, or nearly right, but in context they still made little to no sense. Forget developing a thesis statement, or points of argument, or a compelling conclusion.

What John really loved was cooking. He was creative and innovative in the kitchen; when it came to writing, he tried to be creative, but everything "came out wrong." John and I spent many weeks building his writing skills to the point where he could, near the end of the course, turn in about two pages of writing that made sense structurally but didn't make any compelling point. Before I could make the extremely difficult decision of whether to pass John on to English 100, Composition I, or fail him and ask him to repeat English 098 for another time (or two), he disappeared from class and subsequently dropped out of school a second time. I never saw or heard from him again.

John was something beyond the definition of "basic" writer, as he had not trained to be a writer *at all.* No one had ever sat down with him and looked at his writing; he had been shuttled into a vocational school partly because he loved to cook and loved that kind of creative construction and partly because he had great difficulty with writing (and, to a great extent, reading). John made it clear that he had never really *written* anything in middle or high school. He had been passed along from grade to grade. And he had come to SCSU primarily because he felt family and peer pressure to "go to college," because in today's economy, that's just what you *do*—even when in possession of valuable nonacademic work skills and doing a job you love.

John was the kind of student who prompts the age-old question *where do I start?* So, at SCSU, I had as most of my class Basic Writer Type #3, the linguistically underprepared student in need of pure *grammar* instruction but possessing ideas and known in rubrics as "not competent" or "lacking control of language," and Basic Writer Type #4, also known as "fundamentally deficient" in most rubrics and placed by many teachers, administrators, and others (such as government policy makers) in the more pejorative category "not college material."

I offer these four types of writers to provide an autobiographical rationale for this decidedly historical book. As an experienced teacher of basic writing, I have come to question, through these diametrically opposed classrooms, students, and occasions, what "basic" really means in today's university. I first began to ponder this issue when I was teaching at Michigan as I wondered, "What's really *basic* about these students? Their fears? Their apprehensions? Their self-definitions as *different*—that is, ESL, lower financial class—from their mainstream classmates?"

When I arrived at SCSU, I thought that I had now stumbled upon what "basic" writers *really* were—as I had always been told that as a nonselective institution, SCSU was the kind of place where basic writers *usually* enrolled. But then confusingly enough, other students came along who more closely resembled my Michigan students (especially the ESL students *and* the native speakers who simply did poorly on the entrance exam, without proper time to revise or proofread their work). In yet further semesters, I encountered a few students who more closely resembled those at UIC—students whose secondary schools limited not just *how* they wrote but what *topics* they could interrogate (and even, in some cases, what words they could use to do so—or. rather, what words they were *forbidden* to use, such as *I*). With these constant variables (a deliberate contradiction in terms, I know) for basic writers, both past and present, I just couldn't get a handle on what to expect in my classes—or, importantly, *why*. And when part-time faculty whom I was supervising, as the writing-program administrator (WPA) for the program, asked about how to approach our "remedial" course and its students, I couldn't provide much *guidance* at all—because, depending on the semester, their class might be exceptionally fluid and prepared, or exceptionally limited and underprepared, or somewhere in between.

To complicate matters more, each of the three institutions where I had taught held three very different attitudes toward the basic writing course. At UIC, many of the basic writers were served by the summer version of English 150 (though the course also ran during the regular academic year). A great deal of effort was put into helping these writers gain ground *before* college began; if that could not happen, the course still carried academic credit during the year and was taught by one of the senior lecturers with expertise in basic writing. Students were placed into the course via a standardized, fifty-minute essay exam on one of two reading prompts (which had been unchanged from the time I began directing placement ten years before as an advanced graduate student). Still, the exams were read, in assessment lingo, "supportively," and every effort was made to place students into the standard composition course, English 160. In addition, students with ESL interference markers of note—those that impeded meaning—were placed into English 152, the first-semester course for second-language writers, taught by an ESL specialist from among the lecturer pool.

At Michigan, students were given greater agency over their course work, as they were placing *themselves* into either ECB 100 or ENG 125 or one of the other first-year designated writing courses across the curriculum. The course was credit bearing, if only for *two* credits rather than the standard three credits assigned to the standard first-year writing courses. The classes were small and held in one of the first computerized classrooms on campus; the lecturers assigned to ECB 100 had private office space in the writing center and were encouraged to conduct the class as a semester-long rotation between conferences and workshops,. No one at Michigan ever called ECB 100 "basic writing" (at least not out loud), but it was clearly the course of choice for "basic writers" in the self-placement rubric. In addition, students from the engineering college heavily populated the course, told by their advisors that it was the "right" course for them, regardless of how they answered the placement intake questionnaire.

Finally, at SCSU, basic writing students were placed by a traditional essay exam, much like UIC's but with greater variety in prompts, and were given *zero* credit toward graduation for the course. English 098 focused on academic writing and development of argument. It was not the "drill and skill" course many faculty envisioned that it was—or should be—in an institution such as SCSU. These classes were still small but were often taught by part-time faculty inexperienced in the nuances of modern basic writing instruction or who were coming from area community colleges, where basic writing was envisioned as yet *another* venue—as a sentence-level, paragraph-combining course for students who, most likely, were closer to Basic Writer Type #4. As a result, for several years after my hire, basic writing at SCSU struggled to find its unique mission and pedagogy; only since 2005, for example, has the course been credit bearing.

Given my variable and varied encounters with these students—and the institutions that have declared them "basic"—I have come to this book wanting to posit some lingering, nagging questions about basic writing. First, who *are* basic writers? Second, what role does the social history and mission of a college or university play in determining the answer to this question? Another way of asking these questions is to posit that, if there *is* a universal need, an agreed-upon societal and institutional demarcation for "basic" writers that diagnoses a lack of something specific and transferable from educational site to educational site, then why does the course vary so dramatically from institution to institution?

WHY YALE AND HARVARD?

In 2006, I came upon the means by which I would investigate these questions, as I was reading James Berlin's *Rhetoric and Reality* with a small group of graduate students in an independent study course on composition history and theory. I landed upon the last paragraph of Berlin's fourth chapter, "The Influence of Progressive Education 1920–1940":

> Most students could simply not be expected to meet the complex demands of the rhetorical situations presented in college without additional writing instruction. And this was true not only of the large, democratic state universities but also of the more exclusive schools of the Atlantic seaboard. Yale, for example, in the late twenties introduced a noncredit course called the "Awkward Squad" to provide remedial instruction for those students whose writing in the freshman literature course showed deficiencies (Towle). . . . In his report to the Board of Overseers in 1939, Harvard's president James B. Conant admitted, "From all sides, academic and nonacademic, we hear complaints of the inability of the average graduate to write either correctly or fluently" (qtd. in Wozniak 197). Conant's

> solution was "prescribed work" in the freshman composition class, and in this remedy he was followed by the vast majority of college presidents throughout the country. (91)

The chapter ends there—and Berlin does not again mention the creation of, or the politics surrounding, the presence of "remedial" writing in the Ivy League or in other similarly elite institutions. But this brief mention of Yale's Awkward Squad (and especially its name) stuck with me as I taught my own basic writing students. With all the stigma attached to the designation of "basic"—a stigma that followed the students at each institution where I taught—I began to wonder how and why students had been similarly designated "basic" at one of the most elite institutions in the country, Yale University. Perhaps researching this history would help me to more clearly see "basic" in a cross-institutional and cross-demographic context—as well as a historical one. In my previous work in composition studies, I found no research into the history of basic writing that predated the work of Mina Shaughnessy at City University in the 1970s.

So even though I had not used archival materials in any of my scholarship prior to this time, nor had I been trained in the use of university archives, I decided to go to the Yale to follow the Awkward Squad's winding, hidden path—starting with the references Berlin used, Carroll S. Towle and John Wozniak, and continuing with more research into the course and its creation—through historical documents and other contemporary articles on basic writing from the 1920s through the late 1950s.[1] In doing so, the seeds of this book were planted and grew to include a comparative study of Harvard and its basic writing course during this period. In committing to this often difficult and slippery research—wherein various historical characters emerge via only the most fragmentary pieces of curricular evidence, and leaps of faith and logic must be taken in order to find the documents that hide, buried under unexpected classifications or otherwise benign collections—I have begun to address my questions about the designation and classification of basic writing studies. But I have done so in ways that I did not initially expect, which leads me to ask my readers not only to consider my claims but also to respond to them with additional contextual and historical studies of their own.

Namely, I now believe—and hope through this book to illustrate for other scholars and teachers—that basic writing is *exclusively* an institutional construct, a locally specific course designation that stems from, develops from, and ends with the unique culture of each institution. Through researching basic writing at *elite* institutions, a site long ignored by basic writing historians for reasons that are not entirely surprising, I have found that we cannot fairly label the course "remedial" if, as has clearly been the case, even the "best" students in the country are enrolling in it, because *their* institution of choice has labeled them "not ready" for what first-year writing entails at that location.

I have selected Yale and Harvard as the primary examples for my study for several reasons. First, Yale is a key reference not only for Berlin but also for the pejorative label of "Awkward Squad." Second, to study Yale leads one also to study Harvard—Yale's economic competitor as well as elite rival in the social arena of higher education. Yale and Harvard are a competitive pair—an academic celebrity couple in the throes of a torturous public romance, if you will. To examine basic writing at Harvard and Yale is to challenge the association of *basic* with poorly funded institutions and poorly prepared students and thus as heavily implicated in the *business* of academia. Finally, while Harvard has often been a site for the study of first-year writing, no research of note has investigated its *basic*-writing histories, and this, to me, is a glaring omission in the scholarship of the field. In sum, my use of Yale and Harvard is an attempt to overturn "safe" research designations where basic writing and basic writers are concerned.

In researching these two institutions' writing program histories and writing this book, I have found that we cannot limit the chronological definition of—or research into—basic writing by the research study most popular and widely read in this area, Shaughnessy's 1977 *Errors and Expectations: A Guide for the Teacher of Basic Writing.* I have invoked Shaughnessy in my title to recover some of the history of basic writing *before* her work, a history rarely questioned in the ways I propose here. In situations such as those discussed more fully in chapter 2, Shaughnessy's book limits one's ability to see basic writing *throughout* the twentieth century, as opposed to just post–open admissions in the late 1960s and early 1970s. While we cannot deny the legitimate presence of basic writers in open admissions institutions for these last thirty-five to forty years, we similarly cannot deny the presence of the earlier basic writers who lived and studied (and struggled) prior to this cohort.

My student John is someone who probably would have been in one of Shaughnessy's City University of New York (CUNY) courses, and her efforts to work slowly and methodically through his errors and assumptions about writing may very well have paid off. But the students who populated the remedial writing courses at Yale and Harvard in many ways looked nothing like John and would have found Shaughnessy's methodologies likely at odds with not only their own writing problems but also their own social conditioning as writers and elite young men, bound for well-heeled economic futures. Nevertheless, these students were "basic" in modern, Shaughnessy terms and "remedial" to their contemporaries. Because they lived and wrote before Shaughnessy linguistically reconstituted their academic status and intellectual situation for the field of composition studies does not mean that they should be excluded from research.

This book endeavors to uncover the quiet and pervasive history of basic writing prior to 1960—particularly at elite institutions, specifically Ivy League universities such as Yale and Harvard, and to greatly broaden the definition of *basic writer* so as to ultimately question the usefulness and applicability of this term in today's writing programs. Even though scholars such as Laura Gray-Rosendale[2] have recently argued that defining who the basic writer *is* is less important than what the basic writer *does*, I argue that this distinction between *who* and *what* is almost always made within a particular socioeconomic and/or cultural context and as a means of looking forward into the future populations of basic writing courses rather than into past students and their curriculum.

In the chapters that follow, I make the argument that basic writers can and do exist across institutional types and diverse student populations, based on the configuration and standards of the local writing program, and that the prevalence of these writers has existed far more *historically* than generally acknowledged. Yale and Harvard are two sample case studies that show basic writing courses were alive and well, even in the Ivy League, starting just prior to the 1920s. The widespread institutional disregard for basic writers prevalent on some campuses today began in the early twentieth century as institutions across the country were struggling with the new first-year writing course and with new populations of students occupying or being excluded from that course.

While uncovering this early history of basic writing at elite institutions, I argue that the politics of access and the function of "social sorting" (Fox 54) are not post-Shaughnessy phenomena. Rather, these processes have been at work since the advent of English A at Harvard and the heightened consumer-based policies that resulted in the new admissions criteria of the early twentieth-century American university. In recognizing this long-standing reality of basic writing, we must now reconsider whether the nearly standardized, nationalized definition of "basic" is any longer a beneficial one for the positive growth and democratic development of first-year writing programs and students.

This book is divided into six chapters. Chapter 1 interrogates the concept of "location" through the comparative lenses of real estate and the varied valuations of "place" that may be readily transferred to discussions of first-year writing programs. Specifically, I argue that the first-year writing program is entirely dependent upon how its intellectual location is constructed by the university and how that university's measurements and assessment mechanisms for first-year writers shape the curriculum far more than do the students themselves or their abilities. Thus, the institution's acculturative priorities are highly relevant to first-year composition as the initial location wherein students are stratified and classified as writers or writer types.

Chapter 2 situates the theoretical concept of "basic" in context, specifically reviewing previous scholarship on the definition of the basic writer and the parameters for those students designated as underprepared and questioning how these definitions change when such parameters are complicated by the presence of an elite institutional setting. I argue that, as Bruce Horner notes, the histories of "basic" and "remedial" fail to intersect in the field's literature, thus limiting how we currently define and regard basic writers as we lack a true historical trajectory for this subfield of composition and rhetoric. Were we to expand the definition of *basic* to include a greater historical timeline, we would see that the term has been so variously defined throughout the twentieth century as to be virtually useless as a universal classification.

Chapter 3 examines how the larger discussion of basic writers and basic writing programs influenced the growth of basic writing courses from the 1920s through the 1950s through articles published in issues of *English Journal*, *College English*, and *College Composition and Communication*. These publications in their early years served as forums for opinion pieces and descriptive essays (such as program overviews and teaching strategies), rather than the theoretical or research-based arguments common today. Therefore, they are excellent archival barometers for how basic writing was perceived during this era. I survey these publications to examine not only the ways in which remedial writers were described but also how these writers were comparatively classified, how they were taught (as described by journal authors), and how they were regarded within their institutions and between institutional types. This chapter lays the historical context for the book's next two chapters, which focus on two Ivy League basic writing programs' histories and practices prior to 1960.

Chapters 4 and 5 apply these historical factors of place, definition, and institutional status/selectivity to studies of Yale and Harvard universities, documenting archival evidence of basic writing curricula at these institutions from the 1910s through the mid-1950s. Yale's course grew out of the institution's privileging of literary analysis over rhetorical studies, and school administrators resisted declaring expository writing as a "legitimate" course at the first-year level. In contrast, Harvard's course grew from a post-hoc assessment of student skills in English A, allowing for the rapid development of remedial courses designed to prescribe "fatherly" instruction designed to produce more acculturated men (and writers). Details of the curriculum for both Yale's "Awkward Squad" and Harvard's English C, D, and F show how even though Yale and Harvard both assessed their "basic" writers after they were already enrolled in the standard first-year course, the approach to basic writing at these two institutions differed considerably. True to its more progressive roots, Harvard's remedial writing offerings were in general more universally accepted and more rigorously promoted by students and faculty alike and therefore less stigmatized than the basic writing course offered at Yale, wherein literary values in every case overrode the valuation of expository writing in the first-year classroom.

Finally, chapter 6 posits the concept of a future without official designations of "basic" writing in first-year programs and how the elimination of such a designation would sublimate national and local governmental standards for educational outcomes, including but not limited to the controversial Spellings Report, as each seeks to define high school English curricula and subsequently threatens to negatively affect college writing programs. I propose that even though there are certainly students across the country who are "underprepared" in any variety of ways, we must reconsider whether the need to label students as "basic" outweighs the continued stigma associated with these students and the courses in which they are placed. I argue, ultimately, for a shift in program design that does not eliminate necessary assistance for these writers but also does not rhetorically separate them from other writers in the university or imply that their needs are universal or identical from institution to institution.

1

Locating First-Year Composition

> More than any other college subject, composition has been shaped by perceived social and cultural needs; less than any other college subject it has been informed by a genuine body of knowledge crying out to be disseminated. As a result, we need to examine American culture as it surrounded and shaped college rhetoric, and the economic and ideological forces that this culture brought to bear on the teaching of writing.
>
> —Robert Connors, *Composition-Rhetoric: Backgrounds, Theory, and Pedagogy*

IN THE REAL ESTATE BUSINESS, there is a mantra that controls the fate of all properties: *location, location, location.*[1] No one wants to live next to a toxic-waste dump, no matter how beautiful, new, or stylistically unique the property. If a house is bound to a physical location that raises concern, that property is going to be hard to "move," in real estate parlance. This mantra is closely connected to social and cultural values, especially those concerning one's alignment with the home-ownership *status quo.* Even if a buyer who wouldn't mind living near a huge blinking billboard might still wonder, "What *will* Aunt Susan (or neighbor John or Professor Sam) say when she comes to visit?" Worse yet, the real estate agent counseling the buyer might raise issues of the future of resale. *You* don't mind that big, permanent, six-foot-high pink-pig sculpture in your next-door neighbor's yard, but the *next* buyer surely will. In other words, sometimes location isn't just about the general material conditions of a physical place; it is also about the sociopsychological associations *with* that place and the greater concern for how that place, space, or setting (as each of these subconcepts may have varied weights in any given property) is valued by the community in which the buyer operates.

Location can be seen in more complicated ways than just desirable versus undesirable spaces. Take two identically designed homes but in two very different geographic spaces. Buyer A, who values and desires a house in a quiet, secluded setting, will seek out the house located in the country; Buyer B, who values living near the center of things and desires a short commute, will seek out the house located in the city. Neither of these buyers will be happy with the other's property, even though both locales are reasonably "good" to the average citizen. Both properties will thus appear equally "valuable" in terms of the overall market; however, each will gain a particular buyer based on notions of value that transcend any generic classification that any one agent can create. Location, therefore, is not only about the extreme ends of geographical value or innate "quality" measurements; it is about the particular needs of the individual and how those needs match up to the property being offered or, in the case of composition studies, the local first-year program being designed and delivered to a particular group of students.

With this analogy, I seek to invoke the argument of Peter Vandenberg, Sue Hum, and Jennifer Clary-Lemon that location, in recent scholarship of the field, stands for "the interdependence or mutual reciprocity between people *in* the material and conceptual spaces they occupy" (14). This theory of location is endemic to the first-year writing course—which in composition and rhetoric's history is in a specifically political "location" very much rooted in social interactions between "neighbors" (majors, divisions, schools, and individual institutions' notions of the "value" of writing) and the values students bring to writing These interactions control the way in which writing is taught and, importantly, delivered to first-year students. Sharon Crowley argues that as the only universally required course in the university, first-year composition occupies a powerful role in socializing students to the ways and means of the academy. She argues that despite this reality, "composition scholarship and lore often proceed as if the politics of class, status, and location were not operative in our classrooms" (222). Crowley explains that first-year composition is situated deeply within a politics of place—highly dependent upon the perceived social standing of the larger institution itself:

> The politics of class and location are complicated by two well-established hierarchies that operate among and within institutions: a ranking hierarchy distinguishes worse from better kinds of institutions, and a status hierarchy distinguishes privileged teachers and students from those who are less so. . . . The status hierarchy that operates among disciplines places the sciences at the top; composition is at the bottom. This complex intertwining of privilege, rank, and status explains why composition is not required or taught at older, private, eastern universities; their students (by virtue of native intelligence? Class affiliation? Family connections?) are assumed not to need it. (222)

While it is far from breaking news to note that eastern universities—including Ivy League institutions—are at the top of the American academic hierarchy (both socially and, so our culture believes and endorses, intellectually), it is pertinent to remind ourselves that this status nearly automatically knocks Ivy League students out of eligibility for basic writing instruction. Kathleen Blake Yancey echoes Crowley's theory when she notes that college in general and first-year composition specifically have historically contributed to "normalizing identity" for students—and that such normalizing practices still exist, regardless of where composition occurs or with what means of delivery (2). As such, the elite students enrolled at Ivy League institutions and other comparable locations—who are "prenormalized," if you will—are imagined to have far less need for the induction process offered by first-year composition and certainly assumedly *zero* need for the *pre*normalization of basic writing.

Location also controls other material conditions relevant to composition, such as budgeting, staffing, and physical space within the humanities or liberal arts buildings, as well as psychic or intellectual space within the larger university itself. Thus, one cannot speak about composition at the first-year level as if it were always a static, universal course common to all institutional types and all institutional missions, or as if it were a compartmentalized product that can be moved from place to place without regard for deep and sometimes difficult pedagogical revision.

For example, in the Connecticut state system, where I previously taught, there is a uniform composition course sequence at the community college level but distinctly different course sequences (in course structure and content as well as placement and assessment methodologies) across the four state regional universities. The community college architecture attempts to standardize the curriculum at the general-education level in order to ensure a uniformity of instruction across the twenty or so public community colleges and within the associate degrees granted at those colleges. But when students transfer between the four-year campuses, such idealized uniformity is lost. On the positive side, this lack of uniformity allows each campus to put its personal stamp on the composition course sequence, based on the needs of its student population. At one campus, this means requiring a creative writing course as the second-semester writing offering, in lieu of the more traditional research-based expository course offered at my previous campus. At the other two campuses, there is no second-semester course at all, privileging a more compressed version of composition and a greater attention to upper-division writing among disciplines. The practical downside to this campus-specific personalization within a larger system is obvious: Students who transfer between campuses often "repeat" required courses and become frustrated with the local values that require that they do so. They often asked me, as the WPA, "Why aren't you all the *same?*"

Other state systems, in contrast, have a uniform course sequence—including course name and number—across *all* state institutions (two year and four year) and thus a highly streamlined transfer system for students. While this common course numbering is a unified system of delivery, it discounts the concept of locally specific instructional needs and collapses distinctions between the more prestigious, selective, research institutions in the system and the open-admissions, two-year schools far below in terms of admissions criteria, student-selectivity ratings, and funding status. Perhaps, this equalization is a good thing in some ways, for it allows no one campus to lay claim to the "best" composition course. And, certainly, this transferability has its obvious advantages—as a WPA, I recognize those tangible advantages and see the way in which this type of system can help transfer students complete their degrees more quickly and cheaply. But as a writing teacher and composition studies scholar who cannot forget that critical guiding concept of *location*, such ease of movement, with its erasure of difference, while attractive and even egalitarian, is also deeply troubling.

Such uniformity is troubling because it does not take into account the specifically local needs of any of the individual institutions, the myriad values and preparations of the students attending—and moving between—those institutions, or the local social, economic, and political conditions within which those institutions operate and students come to receive instruction in writing. We would never claim that a house by the nuclear-power plant is equally as valuable as the same house by the attractive, new public park. Similarly, we should never claim that a composition course taught at an elite, selective, four-year institution is equally as "valuable" than an analogous course taught at, say, a two-year community college. But, increasingly, as pressure comes at academia from national movements such as the federal No Child Left Behind and like-minded state-level initiatives, those who believe stubbornly in literacy acquisition as not an individual, intimate process but a rote, testable skill succumb to the notion that a composition course *is* a composition course, regardless of where it "lives"—where it was conceived, cultivated, released into the classroom, and absorbed by students.

Uniformity in course design also does not take into account the diverse *histories* of a particular program or its students. Many composition programs build quickly upon new innovations in pedagogy or changing demographics in their local student populations, sometimes for the good but often in ignorance of the original purposes and design of the course-as-artifact as a historical offering that existed in a particular time and space. Additionally, many legislators forget why, in a state system such as Connecticut's and the system in which I teach now, North Carolina, multiple campuses exist in the *first* place—which is to serve local needs, often built upon local histories, and to provide courses and curricula that speak to those needs, even if dong so seems somewhat at odds with more general trends in instruction. In North Carolina alone, the state system consists of sixteen different institutions, including not only regionally based campuses but also targeted-population campuses important to students' identities—such as historically black universities and historically Native American campuses.

Ignoring—or fundamentally rejecting—historical conditions in composition course design is akin to putting up for sale a house that was built in 1920 but rehabbed in 2000 with no acknowledgment of that overhaul in the listing information or the price justification. Would buyers not need to know what the house *has been* in order to fully appreciate what it now purports *to be*? Would the current owners, who undertook these renovations, not need to know something about the architecture of early twentieth-century America in order to know where to begin with renovations—which structural elements are prudent to keep and which are acceptable to lose? Would the future owners not benefit from having a full history of their home, so that when or if further amendments are made, they are done in the context of past "best practices" in that home's evolution?

In sum, location is physical and metaphysical; in the case of composition studies, it is practical and theoretical. As Johnathon Mauk notes, "Like real estate, higher education is promoting, attempting to get students to buy into ideas about place. The ideas have value, and like plots of land, their value is based on an intersection of the material and the conceptual, of the real and the imagined" (198). Mauk argues, "The physical geography of an institution, and the human geography which surrounds and constitutes it, have an impact on the topography of composition courses—and ultimately influence the success (or failure) of pedagogical strategies" (206). Therefore, location, both past and present, should significantly guide any notion of "value" within a curriculum itself. As much as we might want to do so, we cannot ignore that when we deliver our courses to students, we enter a real-market exchange of goods and services, and we must, therefore, be cognizant of how our course/s measure up to the local needs or values of the students. Still, I want to parse out here the more base notion of *value* as a simple economic good versus *value* as a local, individualized concept for any particular institution and its writing program.

First, it's important to point out that I am not speaking of the relative lack of "worth" associated with composition at lower-level or less-prestigious institutions. My aim is not to claim that college composition taught at elite institutions is more "worthy" of our attention, our tax dollars, or our critical study than similar courses taught at open-admissions or lower-tier institutions. I do not aim to stratify levels of worth among types of composition courses to distinguish between the worthiness of basic- versus first- versus second-semester composition, or the relative worth of offering a college-level course in a high-school setting, or in a nontraditional, adult-education program. What this book instead interrogates is the notion of *valuation* at the local level. I ask what values local institutions bring to their composition courses in order to design those courses, specifically their basic writing courses—including the placement and assessment standards associated with the curriculum—in adherence to local priorities, traditions, and institutional needs as well as how institutional histories impact upon the pedagogical trajectory of the courses themselves.

I mean to draw attention to the importance of community—past and present—in constructing the first-year composition sequence as a material good,. In particular, I want to draw attention to the basic writing course—arguably one of the most critical courses in many a student's college career. I also want to interrogate the relative lack of importance that national or even regional values and histories typically play in any single composition course's specific design, measurements, and learning outcomes. If the basic writing course almost invariably exists in a kind of *local vacuum*—relative to the institution's standards itself but not to a supreme standard of "preparedness" common to all institutions—then perhaps the course has outlived its usefulness and needs to be reconsidered.

In order to situate this argument, this chapter invokes three recent books in the field that provide the theoretical starting points for such a curricular exploration of location. I have chosen these studies from among the many interesting and useful inquiries into basic writing students and curricula because they attempt to situate basic writing within a larger social enterprise that invokes the intersection of the real and the imagined—or, more precisely, the person and the person-type about whom scholars often theorize and subsequently strategize. These studies take real individuals and situate them in real places; as such, they provide a good foundation upon which to lay the differently conceptualized historical work that I am doing. These books are Mary Soliday's *The Politics of Remediation: Institutional and Student Needs and Higher Education* (2003), Lisa Ede's *Situating Composition: Composition Studies and the Politics of Location* (2004), and Linda Adler-Kassner and Susanmarie Harrington's *Basic Writing as a Political Act: Public Conversations about Writing and Literacies* (2002).

BASIC WRITING AND LOCAL MATERIAL CONDITIONS

In her introduction to *The Politics of Remediation*, Soliday persuasively argues for the financial and institutional gains brought about by the proliferation of so-called remedial college writing courses:

> First-year writing courses are usually institutionalized to prepare students to enter the liberal arts and professional schools or to enroll in elective courses. For this reason, a longitudinal perspective is critical in shaping a robust politics of access. However, because a long-term view of a student's (or a teacher's) development would also include an examination of how nonlinguistic factors shape educational success or failure, remediation's agency is less important within the politics of access than it may be from a viewpoint shaped by the politics of meaning. (8)

Soliday argues throughout her book for attention to this "politics of meaning"—how basic writing "means" to individual institutions as not just a course but a gateway into college itself, as a marker of social and economic class, and as a transitional element from the high-school setting that both burdens and financially underwrites the larger university. Soliday, however, focuses on those sites wherein researchers typically find large, traditionally defined basic writing populations: open-admissions universities—specifically the City University of New York (the site of Mina Shaughnessy's research). Soliday's study takes a valuable look at how basic writing enacts a variety of political and socioeconomic institutional controversies at CUNY by virtue of its continued existence and thus focuses more distinctly on the conditions of basic writing and its contextual meaning rather than the basic writing students' abilities themselves.

But in terms of its *site* of study, Soliday's project reinforces the assumptions of much basic writing research. Academia, as well as the larger American culture to a great extent, regards CUNY and similar institutions as the *right* or *logical* or *expected* or *natural* place for basic writers to take up residence. And, consequently, it is by the local standards of CUNY and similarly positioned institutions that we construct the publicly conceived defining line—the colloquial lore of "underprepared" versus "prepared" as a national concept as well as an academic one—between "standard" composition students and "basic" writers and the courses they occupy. This constructing has gone on since Mina Shaughnessy's *Errors and Expectations*. We must now look at basic writing far more historically, prior to Shaughnessy's study, which set a chronological placeholder for basic writing research and advocacy.

Indeed, basic writing programs and the students who populate them are frequently considered "natural" occurrences in certain types of settings, especially since open-admissions came to exist; these settings, being the most democratic of spaces (in admissions terms) populate the literature describing and theorizing underprepared first-year writers. Thus, when scholars talk about basic writers as hypothetically occupying other settings—for example, elite institutions—there is immediate resistance. It is difficult for many academics, let alone members of the public, to conceive of "basic" writers in residence at elite institutions, let alone prior to open-admissions. The equation does not compute, much like the image of a shack in Beverly Hills or an English country estate on the South Side of Chicago. We have difficulty reconciling our preconceived notions of *location* for basic writers with their presence in atypical or "unnatural" settings, such as the prestigious, selective academic institution of the "good old days" (read: before women and minorities came to college). We cannot see how such writers got into that place any more than we can see what they were doing or *not* doing once they arrived.

The more critical question that we need to ask, however, is: What *measurement* is in place that results in a student being classified as "basic" in those more elite locations where writing is taught? To bring this back to the metaphor of housing values, a seller cannot even put a house on the market today unless it has a "big kitchen" (which I put in quotes to invoke the reality of its space as well as the ideology of its materialistic, quasi–home cooking values). Yet, in the 1970s, a seller would have had fewer worries about the kitchen but would have had to pay a great deal of attention to the outdoor spaces—the patio, deck, in-ground pool—that emphasized the valuation of the home as recreational yet *out of sight*, pushed into the privacy of the back yard. As sellers now rehab older homes and in some cases make "vintage" the stylistic components of newer ones, a series of competing measurements and historical values such as these are at play.

Such shifting conceptions of locale, or "place," are at stake in Ede's *Situating Composition*—particularly as Ede works to reshape the subplaces and academic categories into which composition students (and faculty) are shuttled from institution to institution. Unfortunately, she posits an almost ethereal notion of location as it intersects with identity, rather than geography. She does not argue for a localized reading of composition programs, as I do. Instead, Ede argues that the separate powers of theory versus practice—and of teaching the components of each—are highly dependent upon the fluid boundaries between physical and psychological locales and the scholarly predecessors in our field whose highly valuable ideas often become overlooked or eradicated as new theories and pedagogies come into fashion and further polarize the field's origins.

> Location is not fixed, and its interests, subjects, social formations and purposes are sometimes in harmony, sometimes in tension, sometimes in conflict. Any location, in other words,

> is multiply constituted and cannot be helpfully characterized as a single place or identity. As a result, issues of power and authority are key to understanding the politics of location, as there is . . . no "place," no location that is without potential dangers as well as benefits. I make this point to emphasize that my inquiry into the politics of location in composition is in no sense a celebration of the local. (28)

Ede's take on the concept of *location* personalizes the term, as she argues that those in privileged places, or higher positions on the educational hierarchy, must be attentive to those for whom scholarship rarely speaks—students, contingent faculty, and those who participate in composition outside academia, such as participants in literacy circles and other groups. As such, her argument conceptualizes location in far more global terms than mine.

While I do not aim to celebrate the local, I do wish to argue for its importance in order to characterize the local composition program in many ways as an embodiment of the values and priorities of the institution itself. Much as Ede argues that location is not "fixed" in a social sense, I also believe that the first-year composition program, as an intellectual and physical location for incoming students to inhabit for one to three semesters (or, in more negative terms, as a "holding tank" for this time), absorbs and reflects what the institution wants its students to *be* and to *have been* prior to admission, not some universal, historical "good." Upon admission to University X, students will need to not only show what they *have done* in secondary school but also predict what they *will do* in the university itself. This prediction is largely based on intake assessments, such as placement testing, but is also based on how successfully other, previous students have worked toward their degrees (or have rejected that path—or had the path taken away from them through failure); and how much the institution wants the incoming student to accomplish in the four, five, or six years s/he will be enrolled. First-year composition is certainly about an institution's valuation of literacy—as it is locally defined—but it is also about meeting and exceeding predictors for student success, based on an estimation of how many semesters a student should be held in writing courses and how those writing courses should be stratified. The better the predictors, the more likely the student writer will emerge as a "finished" product meeting the literacy values of the local institution. And the more finished the students, the more the program and institution will be perceived as a successful, legitimate location for pursuing and obtaining a college degree.

Ede's list of questions about composition studies as a field is relevant to the notions of place explored here. For example, Ede asks, "Consider the following potential starting points for a genealogy of composition. What do these various locations expose or repress? Fifth century Greece? Harvard in the 1890s? The first meeting of the Conference on College Composition and Communication held at the Stevens Hotel in Chicago in 1950?" (4). Similarly, Ede raises issues that intersect with other issues of literal, physical "origins" for composition:

> What structures of desire and resistance circulate in composition? What is the relationship, for instance, between composition's desire for professional legitimacy and disciplinary status and its curricular positioning in the academy as gatekeeper and certifier? Between its desire to effect broad social reform and its identification in both popular and academic cultures with linguistic correctness and propriety? (4)

To connect these issues of "correctness and propriety" to the origins of composition is a profitable endeavor when theorizing location in basic writing's current and past institutional practices. Where do we *start* our history of *basic* writing—at or near the first CCCC? Between World Wars I and II, when shifts in enrollments changed the physical landscape of the American college? Or earlier than that—after the first class of first-year English students at Yale included writers with a diagnosed need for more "refinement" in their written literary analyses? Or earlier still, when the first "standard" college composition class, English A, was created in order to correct upperclassmen deficiencies at Harvard—thus repositioning college *composition* as technically *basic* writing from the start? Each of these physical, historical locations says something different about the value and institutional worth of basic writing and basic writing students—and each also aligns itself with an increasingly historical sense of "correctness and propriety," assuming that prior to its inception, student writers were *always* highly literate and *always* "good" at composing texts.

I would argue that first-year student writers' stratification is thus entirely dependent on how the institution determines and defines *readiness* and *proficiency* through its chosen methods of location-specific measurement—whether those be through SAT scores, entrance exams, or other assessment mechanisms (such as the often complex formulas used by admission committees, which take into account social background, extracurricular interests, and family income). Adler-Kassner and Harrington explain in *Basic Writing as a Political Act* that such extracurricular realities are critical in seeing the larger picture of basic writing programs and students. Their arguments

> are grounded in the realities of the constraints in which basic writing researchers, and basic writing students, must operate. To deny that a number of individuals and groups have a vested interest in seeing tangible results stemming from basic writing instruction is to turn a blind eye to the situation in which education currently operates, . . . [yet other] basic writing research positions writers as individuals working outside of social contexts, particularly their own historical contexts. (8–9)

This research, Adler-Kassner and Harrington assert, denies basic writing students any real choice or agency in their own writerly construction. Their description of what constitutes a "basic writer" or, more accurately, of how a basic writer is *constituted* by the typical researcher or research study illustrates that

> whatever the methodology or approach used for such studies, many of them start with an examination of what students *cannot* or *did not do,* thus initially positioning writers outside the author function identified by Foucault and extended to basic writing by Gail Stygall. . . . [W]hen writers are placed outside of the author function from the onset, they are immediately disempowered; they cannot gain the purchase necessary to work against their exclusion. (15)

If we apply this approach to incoming first-year students at the university—which requires "an examination of what students *cannot* or *did not do*"—we can see the role that the local institution plays in determining what type of literacy instruction a student will receive. Such determination is manifest, for example, in the cutoff for a SAT verbal score placing students in basic or developmental courses. Such determination is also manifest in the reading of portfolios or other samples of student writing, which are usually written in a high-school context and then translated to the values of a college setting. Such considerations of intake measurements are important when attempting to break new ground in basic writing research by investigating the more unexpected sites of students forced, by local literacy values, into their roles as "disempowered" writers who cannot participate in true authorship of their own educational futures.[2]

Indeed, Adler-Kassner and Harrington's concept of "objective literacy" is what is truly at stake in an investigation of basic writing and location. The notion of *basic* as an immutable term across all sorts of institutions and institutional levels contradicts the social and economic forces at work in each individual college or university—forces that dictate what and *who* "basic" is, often without regard for how that definition aligns with or contradicts other colleges' or universities' definitions of the same. Adler-Kassner and Harrington believe—and I concur—that "emphasizing the ways that basic writers' processes or texts are marked by difference or deficit implicitly promotes a definition of literacy that is, to some degree, autonomous" (15). We might place a great priority on "benchmarking," for example, our curricula so that courses in writing (and other subjects) *resemble* like-minded courses at other "sister" institutions, but we far less frequently ask ourselves if the prerequisite, entrance exam—or other rubric for that like-minded course—*also* reflects that of other institutions. Further, we even *less* frequently ask whether that rubric or placement mechanism is a *sound* one, given the variability of student ability and need between local settings. In our desire to strengthen our own curricula and, in most cases, to provide the best possible instruction for underprepared writers, we turn a blind eye to the ways in which "literacy" purports to be a universal term, when it is an unstable, fluid concept that merges with the culture and social valuation of each institutional setting.

In the chapters that follow, I continue with the idea of location as a critical factor in shaping first-year writing curricula generally and basic writing courses (and students) specifically. In chapter 2, I seek to connect these complicated factors regarding location and composition studies to the definition of "basic" writing (and basic writers) as a theoretical concept. In doing so, I hope to illustrate how and why such an overarching term, in the context of institutional "place," has both been limited by our field's concentration on under-prepared writers post-open-admissions, and has been overused as a catch-all site for any student who, as determined by local conditions, resides outside the "norm" for college-level literacy.

2

(Re)Defining *Basic* in Context

> At least half of higher education is a matter of selecting, sorting, and classifying students.
>
> —James Bryant Conant, Harvard University president 1933–53, February 1938

LOCATING BASIC WRITERS IN composition studies scholarship historically has been a fairly narrow query, in socioeconomic terms. The prevailing argument has been that basic writers have existed most visibly in the least-prestigious institutions and are most represented among the least-prepared, ergo financially or socioeconomically disadvantaged, students. Since the 1970s, composition studies has advocated for the institutional welfare of developmental writers from these underrepresented groups in academia, most famously at open-admission institutions such as the City University of New York (CUNY), the site of Mina Shaughnessy's influential 1977 study *Errors and Expectations*. Shaughnessy's book reified the pedagogy and, by extension, the politics of the basic writing classroom, by classifying the basic writer not as *deficient* but as *underprepared*. This move shifts the origins of the teaching problem from the students themselves (and their own intellectual motivation) to the cultures and communities in which they were schooled. Such a shift rejects the edict to "make up" neglected skills in favor of declaring these skills as never having been presented to the students in the first place. This important shift in attitudes has helped many students where previously they would have been allowed to fail. In the long shadow of Shaughnessy's legacy, however, composition studies has continued to operate under the assumption that basic writers such as the ones Shaughnessy worked with at CUNY—with their particular error patterns, alternate literacies, and sociocultural markers—are not only the most deserving of our advocacy but are also the benchmark by which we define *basic.*

In order to overturn this assumption, we must accept two realities that describe the state of basic writing studies in the twenty-first century. These are, first, that basic writing is a false historical marker that, instead of renaming a sort of student who has attended U.S. colleges for one hundred years, purports that such students are new to first-year writing programs, and, second, that *basic writing* is a *relative* term, meaning something different in context as it is transferred from the open-admissions location of Shaughnessy to other institutions. As argued in chapter 1, the primacy of location cuts both ways. Inasmuch as composition programs need to privilege their institutional histories and local values when designing curricula and standards for preparedness, so, too, must elite or more selective universities that "locate" a proportion of their students as basic writers be regarded as sites for the localized study of basic writers.

BASIC WRITING: A FALSE HISTORICAL MARKER

Jeanne Gunner notes in "Iconic Discourse: The Troubling Legacy of Mina Shaughnessy" that Shaughnessy is consistently "posited as the starting point from which later ideas flow and to whom they are attributed, not necessarily conceptually, but always relationally" (28). As a result, Gunner argues, Shaughnessy's legacy inhabits the author function of impeding the field's ability to move past a definition of basic writing and basic writers that is both "site-specific and site-iconic" (30). Joseph Harris takes this one step further in *A Teaching Subject: Composition since 1966* by arguing that Shaughnessy is "less of an advocate of a position which many people might now find compelling than [a] kind of icon" (77). Harris says that even though Shaughnessy positioned herself as an "amateur and reformer" in the pedagogy of basic writing, the "frontier" that she "claimed to have stumbled upon was already quite well developed" (79). Prior to the early 1970s, basic writing lacked the professional markers of a subfield—most notably the scholarship on basic writing theory and practice now found in professional journals. Basic writing prior to Shaughnessy was also not yet deemed "basic"—because this term was coined by Shaughnessy, replacing *remedial* and other terms (including but not limited to *corrective*, *hospital*, *bonehead*, and *zero* English). Yet, Harris notes, Shaughnessy's landmark study and her subsequent iconic status have not only brought more attention to basic writers as a field of study (a positive) but also, unfortunately, effectively erased the history of basic writers and writing programs that existed before CUNY.

I agree that Shaughnessy's association with the forward-reaching field of basic writing has obscured the deeper chronological history of the basic writer, impeding any competing study of her institutional histories and this subfield's more varied constituencies. It is time to reach back into those histories in order to reset the definition of basic writing both chronologically and conceptually to include basic writers whose institutional identities have been erased or dramatically minimized. Shaughnessy's legacy has taken the field forward into new theories of basic writing, positioning the start date of basic writing advocacy and research as the early 1970s, following open admissions and the influx of women and racial minorities into colleges and universities. The larger history of rhetoric and composition has been examined via the archival work of Albert R. Kitzhaber, James Berlin, Robert Connors, Sharon Crowley, and David Jolliffe, among others, and through textual studies of composition-related materials from the nineteenth and twentieth centuries by scholars such as Marolina Salvatori, Jean Ferguson Carr, John Brereton, and Patricia Donahue and Gretchen Fleisher Moon.

But composition studies has yet to reexamine within this larger history how *basic writing* and its students were classified and received prior to the 1970s. Shaughnessy's work has allowed holistic reconsideration of the pejorative face of basic writing post–open admissions and the pedagogy that has evolved alongside the critical diversification of the student body. But in order to fully grasp the social history and future consequences of basic writing studies, we must revisit earlier institutional groupings of underprepared writers, especially those overlooked by the current standards of "basic" due to their privileged socioeconomic standing.

The limited, available histories of basic writing as a subfield within composition studies and of basic writers as a sizeable population in both public and private universities prior to open admissions serve as textual witness to this iconic link between Shaughnessy and *Errors and Expectations* and the larger construction of basic writing studies. Andrea Lunsford's dissertation, one of the few book-length studies to include a discussion of basic writing's early history, credits Shaughnessy with beginning the critical conversation about basic writers. Lunsford notes that at the time of her writing (1977), there had been little critical examination of remedial writing save Shaughnessy, who "has been studying the writing of remedial students and pointing [out] the need for more and better research since at least 1973" (13). Following Shaughnessy's lead, Lunsford's dissertation aims to "set the current hue-and-cry into historical perspective and to evaluate past as well as present responses to remedial students" (13). Lunsford then interrogates possible alternate terms for *remedial*, including "new; disadvantaged; handicapped; nontraditional; developmental; marginal; high-risk; basic; compensatory" (14). She notes that *remedial* implies something "affording remedy, tending to remedy something" (15) yet settles on this term for her study, partially due to Shaughnessy's argument that "all other terms tend to translate into remedial 'when the chips are down'" (qtd. in Lunsford 20).

Lunsford herself went on to make invaluable contributions to the subfield of basic writing and to the larger field of rhetoric and composition studies. Since her dissertation came directly on the heels of *Errors and Expectations*, it is fitting that Lunsford gave that book its historical and professional due. I do not mean to critique Lunsford's motives for following Shaughnessy's lead, yet it is interesting how heavily indebted her work is to Shaughnessy even as she simultaneously uncovers prior historical evidence of basic writing in American universities. For example, her second chapter is devoted almost entirely to reviewing the then-current debates over basic literacy in the context of remedial writing instruction prior to the 1970s, citing scholars such as Kitzhaber as well as historical sources such as William Riley Parker and Adams Sherman Hill. In beginning to demonstrate the long-standing debate over writing standards and definitions of *remedial* from as early as the turn of the last century, Lunsford determines that some generalizations may be made about basic writing instruction. These generalizations are that courses were noncredit and "punitive in nature"; were mostly "drills and exercises"; positioned students as "lazy or stupid—or both"; and were taught by "totally or largely unprepared" teachers who would rather be "lecturing on moral excellence or on a favorite work of literature" (41–42). Lunsford further cites evidence of remedial courses in place at elite institutions such as Wellesley College at the end of the nineteenth century (40). In this context, she also mentions Paula Johnson's study of Yale's "Awkward Squad" (41).

Lunsford presents her historical research as a preamble to her focus on basic writers at the Ohio State University. What is striking, then, is that her historical survey has stood virtually alone for these past thirty years, with no significant scholarly follow-up or response. William DeGenaro also noted this absence of scholarship supporting or responding to Lunsford's dissertation, questioning why "in an age marked by regressive social policies and unchecked elitism within all levels of public education are practitioners and scholars of basic writing largely ahistorical?" (54).

In "The History of Composition: Reclaiming Our Lost Generations," Robin Varnum echoes this lament regarding the tendency of composition scholars to overlook the first half of the twentieth century, noting that Stephen North "has chosen to date the birth of [composition studies] to 1963, as if nothing before that were worth talking about" (39). Varnum argues that "the sixty years between roughly 1900 and 1960 have been characterized as a period of stagnation in the history of composition" (40). Viewing the early years of composition in such a broadly negative manner, Varnum argues, has had "the effect of denying the resources and lessons of portions of the past to many of us currently teaching composition" (40). Sample questions to which we do not have answers for this particular time period include: "Who learned to write? How many of them were there? How much did their teachers get paid?" (Varnum 40).

Such calls to uncover composition's origins have not gone completely unheeded, as composition and rhetoric scholars have begun to visit the archives in order to answer some of the questions posed by Varnum.[1] As a result, an even greater proliferation of composition's history has occurred and is frequently as seen through gendered or other sociotheoretical lenses. But for *basic* writing's "early" scholarship and history, researchers still repeatedly circle back to Shaughnessy, thirty years after *Errors* made its mark on this area of composition studies. Why is this the case?

Despite her long-standing and generally positive influence on basic writing pedagogy, Shaughnessy has not been without her critics. Patricia McAlexander states that Shaughnessy's work "is not evaluated as objectively as it should be" (29), since her characterization of basic writers as students "striving heroically to overcome their Victimization" is so politically compelling (35).[2] Similarly, Deborah Mutnick claims that Shaughnessy's work inadvertently "helped construct a category of basic writer based on deficient, if logical, language use" and that Shaughnessy gave us collateral labels for basic writers, among them "true outsiders" who are "strangers in academia" (33). Shaughnessy's definition of *basic* refers as much to the social standing of the person in relation to the institution as it does to the student's skills themselves. For Shaughnessy and those scholars—most notably, David Bartholomae and Patricia Bizzell—who have subscribed to her theories and advanced them into work on student acculturation, basic writers need "accommodation" without fearing that such accommodation will "weaken their existing relationship with their home cultures" (Lu 890). In such a paradigm, basic writers are perpetually outsiders seeking a way into the world of academia—a world which is socially and demographically so much unlike their own.

That basic writers are primarily (or exclusively) "strangers" to academia is a compelling theory and a stance that allows such students fitting this social classification to find a physical and intellectual place of their own inside the often-foreboding institutional gates. Yet, this theory is limited in light of what we now know about language acquisition and the role of socialization in the writing process, as well as in light of the appearance historically of more elite students—as defined socially and economically—in basic writing courses. If we continue to classify the whole of underprepared writers as "strangers," it is almost impossible for us to recognize and assist basic writers who emerge from other populations assumedly "familiar" with academic discourse and intellectual conventions.

If we define *all* basic writers, per David Bartholomae, as those who have yet to "invent" the university for their own intellectual purposes, we discount the presence of otherwise well-prepared students who are classified as "not ready" for the work facing them in their own institution's first-year writing classroom. As Neal Lerner notes in his study of the mid-twentieth-century demise of the Dartmouth Writing Clinic, elite institutions throughout the twentieth century "have also experienced [the] struggle" of assisting and intellectually integrating such students (14). Lerner states that in order to maintain their "brand," or public marker of capital as an elite institution, such schools, including Dartmouth, have sought to protect their reputation "from the uncomfortable reality of student performance" and particularly from the work of under-prepared student writers (14). As Lerner adeptly illustrates with this Dartmouth example, the "outsider" label may not be sufficient in regarding atypical, socially elite students who are also, on their campuses, basic writers.[3]

Another scholar who has brought to light the problematic historical dimensions of Shaughnessy's work is Bruce Horner. In "Discoursing Basic Writing, " Horner argues that Shaughnessy's work delineated *basic* from the earlier *remedial* so absolutely that it caused the field to eschew these earlier students (and classifications) in favor of the "new frontier" of more "strategic uses" in program advocacy and the field's professionalization (211). In addition to declaring that the new term *basic* almost always referred to minority students, at least in the case of CUNY, Horner argues that positioning "basic writing and basic writing students as 'new' and 'beginning' erases the ties of both to history and society" (212).

> Constructing Basic Writing as a "pedagogical West" has prevented teachers and administrators of basic writing from learning past endeavors. As critics have begun to point out, the

> history of remedial writing instruction, though not labeled "basic writing," began long before the 1970s (Connors, Lunsford, Rose). Acknowledging the history of remedial writing instruction would not only enable teachers "not to make the same old mistakes over and over again" (Lunsford 252); it would enable them to counter damaging representations of their own work and their own students as temporary, marginal, and therefore easily expendable. The divorce of Basic Writing from the history of "remedial" writing instruction effected by its claims to "newness" has prevented teachers from arguing for the historical centrality of their teaching of writing. (211)

Highlighting several of Horner's terms here is particularly fruitful for a discussion of little-known basic writing populations, such as Ivy League students. Horner's notion of a "claim to newness" is especially compelling, as it highlights the ever-present problems of historicizing a field constantly in transition. We are loathe to recall our earlier, less-informed, remedial writing pedagogies, certainly in part because we believe we have come so far from these methodologies. Horner argues that we artificially separate the post-1970 students known as "basic" writers from the pre-1970s students known as "remedial" writers. In doing so, we create an illogical gap between these groups of students, even though their literacy needs and especially their stigmatized position in the curriculum remain quite similar.

Also key to proposing a reification of basic writing research is the notion of a false "temporary . . . and easily expendable" class of basic writers. As chapter 3 illustrates, the prevailing attitude from the 1910s onward among teachers, administrators, and other university officials has been that if only a "solution" could be found to the problem of basic writing (or, to align such thinking with the label of "hospital" English, a "cure"), these writers would *go away.* Importantly, if such a cure were associated with negative outcomes or disincentives—such as extra fees for remedial coursework, non-credit status for basic writing/remedial courses, or damaging labels like "zero English"—surely such students would get their collective act together and just *stop being remedial*. Such disincentives, in Mina Shaughnessy's estimation, amount to the decision of faculty to "[yield] nothing to the inferior preparation of their students (introduction 1.1:2), and, clearly, these poorly rationalized strategies have not, in fact, magically eliminated underprepared students. But, even more clearly, these strategies are far from "new." As Horner asserts, establishing a fuller and more public, scholarly connection between today's basic writers and earlier remedial writers prevents us from imagining that our writing curricula must ceaselessly respond to an "always new" crisis in student preparation.

To accept this earlier history fully and with an open mind, we must recognize that Shaughnessy's important work was only one link in a much-larger chain of basic/remedial writing study and was a definable moment in the movement to further classify writers by ability characteristics so as to find a way to best enable their academic progress. Tom Fox argues that *Errors and Expectations* "embodied *and still* embodies, in an unsurprising way, the tensions of access and inclusion" (45). In *Defending Access: A Critique of Standards in Higher Education*, Fox provides a theoretical framework for employing the early history of basic writing students and curricula pre-Shaughnessy.

> [D]evoid of content, [basic] writing courses become better suited to the task of social sorting. If basic writing programs primarily concern themselves with serving the university, then political questions, or any questions that challenge existing definitions of basic writing, become irrelevant to the bureaucratic task of reproducing the program. (54)

Fox assigns this "social sorting" function to the seemingly inclusionist realm of *initiation theory* in basic writing (56). Chiefly promoted by Bartholomae and Bizzell, initiation theory relies upon the definition of the basic writer as being part of a distinct community that must be initiated into the university; Fox argues that this theory "simplifies both the academic community and the students' communities, representing both as homogeneous and mutually exclusive" (56).

BASIC: A RELATIVE TERM

Lynn Quitman Troyka's 1987 essay, "Defining Basic Writing in Context," serves as an opening query into the relativity of the "basic" writing student within and among institutional contexts. Troyka offers her own students at Queensborough Community College as examples of basic writers who do not seem to be covered/examined in current basic writing scholarship—asserting that the students who are studied in this scholarship are "not the ones [she knows]" (3). In addition, the students whom she teaches are themselves difficult to classify as one "type"—or definition—of basic. As a result, Troyka contends, "For about a decade, the term *basic writing* has been common in our profession. Its definition, however, remains elusive" (2).

Troyka wonders, "Who is and who is not a basic writer?" and cites Shaughnessy's own consideration of the relativity of such labels by reminding readers, "One school's remedial student may be another's regular or even advanced freshman" (qtd. in Shaughnessy, *Errors and Expectations* 4). She uses data from a pilot study of twelve basic writing teachers from across the United States to show the difficulty in classifying one type of basic writer, even using broad divisions such as "high, medium, and low" (11) that separate students by ability levels. In basic writing studies, Troyka ultimately argues, "The bandwagon effect seems to be taking over. The term *basic writing* is applied loosely to various populations of students, thus diminishing the energies we must spend on those students central to our undertaking" (13).

Even though I disagree with what Troyka seems to be arguing for in this conclusion, namely limiting basic writing advocacy to the "true" basic writers—those with the most limited skills and from open-admissions institutions—I do agree that basic writers are a historically diverse group of students who continue to grow in number through a "bandwagon" effect initiated by anxiety-filled institutions who "suffer from too many 'shoulds'" (Troyka 13). As such, Troyka's call to resist an overarching label for basic writers still resonates more than twenty years after her essay was published and in the context of a greater attention to historical institutional bandwagons of similar ilk.

Indeed, Shaughnessy herself, upon founding the *Journal of Basic Writing* in 1975, set a broad, elusive, and cautionary baseline for the definition of "basic." It is fair to say, given the dearth of scholarship on basic writers prior to Shaughnessy's time, that little research on remediation was available at this time. In the introduction to the second issue of that publication, Shaughnessy contextualized her position on basic writing by debunking certain myths of uniformity of instruction that exist behind what historically had been upheld as "standard" versus "basic" designations:

> There was a time in France, we are told, when it was possible to say at any given point during the day what every schoolboy in the country was reading. However enviable such curricular certainty might seem to Basic Writing teachers in this country during these times, it is clearly not at this point remotely possible. As yet, the teaching of writing to under-prepared college freshmen is too loose and unstudied an experience to allow for uniformity even within programs let alone among them. Colleges define "basic" differently, depending on the skills levels of the "regular" students; budgets for basic writing range widely from campus to campus . . . and then there are predilections and resources of individual teachers or program administrators which lead to the choice of one path to competence rather than another. (1)

Such a reminder harkens to Shaughnessy's note in volume 1 of *JBW* that error is "the unintentional deviation from expected patterns" (4). This definition of error, alongside Shaughnessy's own insistence that basic writers are not one set "type," gives a fruitful entrée into seeing basic writers in other atypical contexts, wherein such "deviation" also leads to institutionally specific, relative "basic" labels for some student writers at atypical institutions.

For example, in her 1989 essay "Reexamining Basic Writing: Lessons from Harvard's Basic Writers," Cherryl Armstrong asserts that, based on her experiences teaching Expos 5, the basic or preparatory course at Harvard University, "*basic* is a relative term" (69). Positioning basic writers' work at Harvard against basic writers' work at

California State University at Northridge, Armstrong argues that we must not be too quick to make unilateral statements about what or who "basic" writers are, as there are "common denominators among students in basic courses at all levels" (70), specifically "the limitations of their approaches to writing tasks, what they think about their work, and what they know and do not know about writing" (74). Here, Armstrong makes important observations about the *self-perceptions* of basic writers in relation to the local demands of their university writing programs. In her discussion about situated definitions of "basic," Armstrong also echoes Mike Rose's critical assertion (a part of this scholarly chain that echoes Shaughnessy's initial claims) that "what is remedial for a [research university] might be standard for other state or community colleges, and what is considered standard during one era might well be tagged remedial the next" (Rose, "Language" 349).

On the surface, a call to study basic writers at institutions like Harvard and Yale may puzzle some readers. Why should we care about lesser-prepared Ivy Leaguers when we have so many students struggling academically and financially just to *get by* in our public and/or open-admissions colleges nationwide? Further, are we sure that such a population even *exists* when we consider how basic writers have been typically defined? These are valid questions. As Armstrong herself states, "If you place the words basic writing and Harvard in close proximity, you are likely to attract attention" (68). Like Armstrong, I recognize that examining basic writers in the Ivy League is atypical and thus bound to elicit strong reactions from readers familiar with basic writing studies as it is usually framed. As such, it behooves me to, in Troyka's footsteps, (re)define "basic" in context.

It is true that the main tenet of basic writing pedagogy (and advocacy) is to ensure, first, an egalitarian access to academic literacy for underprepared students within an accessible, affordable institution and, second, a social and cultural mobility for these students that corresponds to the institution's larger mission. Such work rightly aims to give a voice to those who are not part of the upper "classes" of academia,. It is also true that the vast majority of basic writing students whom we encounter in our teaching come from marginalized social or communal spaces, often with literacy values that are in direct conflict with those of academia. These are students at the mercy of university placement systems, national and local standardized tests, and other intake measurements that do little to measure what students *know* but instead how they can *perform* in a depersonalized assessment situation. These are the students who are often delayed in their entrance to credit-bearing writing courses, in hopes that they will give up and disappear from college altogether. In Gail Stygall's words, basic writers are "like boxers who are bleeding and winded but not yet ready to quit" ("Politics and Proof in Basic Writing" 28).

But even as I freely acknowledge these typical conditions for basic writers in our universities, I wish to focus on the larger institutional mechanism at work in first-year composition, regardless of the student(s) or the local setting. This mechanism is simply one of *stratification*, the highly subjective classification and division of students' abilities as they align—or misalign—with the values and objectives of a particular institution. I want to recall, therefore, how and why basic writers have historically existed—and have been stratified—at less-selective *as well as* elite institutions. As Ira Shor has argued, writing courses at the university are products of not only academic/intellectual leveling but also social and cultural discrimination. Shor notes, "Writing instruction's focus on correct usage and academic discourse actually represents a political process where the social construction of people and the larger culture is at stake. . . . Writing's social function is to help reproduce inequality, which requires mass failure to preserve the hierarchies now in place" (30). Filtering Shor's points through the lenses of elite students, specifically those men—almost all Caucasian and upper-middle to upper class—who were enrolled at Yale and Harvard between approximately 1920 and 1960, one can see that Shor's comments, while succinctly representative of the conditions facing traditionally defined basic writing students at non-elite universities, *can* also be applied to early basic writers at these Ivy League institutions. Yale and Harvard's basic writing students during this time period also underwent a "political process" of social construction in that they were marked as "deficient"—in Yale's case via their collective label of the "Awkward Squad" and in Harvard's case through follow-up courses such as English "D," designed for students who received a grade of "D" in the standard first-year writing course, English A.

These students' enrollment in courses designated as remedial slowed their progress and reinforced the hierarchy of sanctioned literacies in the first-year course. Such hierarchical distinctions, coincidentally, were born around the time that Yale, Harvard, and other Ivies began, due to institutional financial exigency, to admit students whom administrators considered "below" their typical or normal standards. While these students were by virtue of admission to a top-tier institution the *elite,* they certainly were not in that context the *norm*. In the case of the Awkward Squad, for example, due to their lack of facility with "correct usage and academic discourse" in literary analysis, a lack that did not correspond with Yale's values, these students were institutionally labeled as remedial.

Although it is still easy to feel fewer sympathies for these elite basic writers, note that when we label any writing course or any writing student "basic" in nature, we are pejoratively marking this curricula or person as outside the mainstream, outside the norm, whatever that norm may be, however it may evolve over time with the values of the institution. It is a dangerous assumption that basic writers *only* exist among traditionally defined sources of "underpreparedness," resulting in this classification becoming universal in its application and post–open admissions in its necessity. Such writers were segregated prior to the 1970s, variously defined as the "subfreshm[a]n, remedial student, developmental student, and nontraditional student" (Jensen 53).

Indeed, the largest problem facing the basic writing student—of past and present, at any institution—is how to become socially and intellectually integrated into the mainstream of his/her institution. As Mary Soliday states, the perception that such intellectual stratification sets political and social boundaries palatable to the tuition-paying public allowed a "set apart" status to become the norm in the early twentieth century. Soliday notes that from 1920 to 1945,

"Remediation . . . helped to solve the crisis inherent in defining what a college education was going to be, who was going to get it, and where it would be offered" (38). This stratification served to further delineate the college experience as only for certain types of students, relegating those on the margins to specialized curricula marking them as deficient. Soliday argues, "We must challenge the rhetoric of needs that assumes remediation is a 'special' need of nontraditional students" (61) in order to fully understand the history of basic writing and its continuing legacy in writing programs.

Soliday also contends that economic conditions factor into how and why remedial programs are offered at the university and that "to gain coveted funding . . . colleges did not reject students but deployed various remedial traditions to establish standards after admission and before graduation" (47). Facing declining enrollments, prestigious institutions lowered their own requirements to gain financially from a population heretofore not allowed admission. This is not to imply, however, that basic writers entering college from 1920 to 1960 were solely the product of new "low" standards. Rather, elite institutions like Harvard and Yale entered into a compromise between their traditionally defined standards and current feasibility. One consequence was a redefinition of their first-year population, including some students who had not until that point been given the opportunity of an Ivy League education, including women and minority populations.

Soliday's confirmation of these historical conditions may be set alongside the work of other scholars who have discussed the position of basic writers versus the accepted "norm," including how and where division and classification of basic writers occur within a first-year curriculum. Mary Sheridan-Rabideau and Gordon Brossell assert that "there is a tremendous range of problems among basic writers, [thus] it would be dangerous to lump all basic writers into one category" (22). More recently, Nancy Sommers's documentary study of Harvard first-year writing students, *Shaped By Writing*, has shown that levels of facility with writing can be quite locally specific—defined by criteria such as difficulty with advancing the meaning of texts or transforming abstract knowledge into dialectical frameworks on the page. Harvard's "basic" writers are thus likely quite adept with the basics of grammar and spelling but in the context of the expectations they face in their university studies still in need of preparatory work in order to enter the local writing arena.

Given that increasingly complex standards of literacy suggest that college is the "new high school" and, further, that first-year composition is, according to scholars such as Margaret Marshall, "the newest level of literary expectation" (3), the segregation of basic writers may now be even more debilitating to the incoming first-year student. As Marshall argues,

> the kinds of literacy taught and practiced even among the most elite has changed over time. Likewise, the availability of higher education to larger segments of the population can be seen as part of a pattern of American ideology that promises rewards based on individual merit, uses literacy abilities to sort these individuals, and fosters increasing levels of education to ensure the status of the middle class. (9)

Such an ideology affects not only the status and preparation of teachers—Marshall's central concern—but also makes the notion of "sorting" a shifting, site- and time-specific concept, a moving target that can be altered at will, much like the overall definition of *literate.*

Additionally, basic writers may be situationally defined and sorted institutionally in terms of who *teaches* them. The common image of the basic writing classroom is an urban setting, filled with first-generation college students as well as nonnative speakers, taught by a part-time or contingent faculty member who, like the students s/he teaches (and this image *is* most often a feminized one), is disenfranchised. For example, in historicizing the professionalization of community-college English faculty between 1950 and 1970, Jeffrey Andelora examines Kitzhaber's 1963 characterization of these faculty as simply overseers of "mechanical drill[s] of the most stupefying kind" (Kitzhaber qtd. in Andelora 9). Andelora notes that these remedial writing teachers, working in community colleges that were under the budgetary control of local school districts and who were mostly former and current high-school teachers, were in Kitzhaber's view "ill-prepared to teach the academic curriculum" (9), a view that offered a top-down, broadly negative perspective on underprepared writers and their concomitant course work. Such a statement harkened back to the push-pull relationship between high-school and college faculty and administrators over who was responsible for the teaching of writing as well as who was qualified to do so, a historical curricular problem explored more in chapter 3.[4]

Alternatively, such faculty are simultaneously viewed by some as the martyrs of higher education. Gunner astutely argues that the basic writing teacher "holds a position of honor" and is "constructed as a kind of hero, one who identifies with and champions basic writers, and who enacts a Virgilian role of guide into academic discourse" (31). Gunner notes that such a teacher is seen as primarily "altruistic" by nature and as working in the service of the "radically democratic" (31).

Gunner's gloss of the prototypical basic writing teacher—one whose construction has been idealized to the point of institutional legend—is one example of the way in which basic writing is impossibly excluded from the halls of elite institutions. Another view of basic writing teachers and status comes from Min-Zhan Lu, who argues persuasively that in Shaughnessy-era basic writing instruction, "any sign of heterogeneity, uncertainty, or instability [was] viewed as problematic" (895) and thus that teachers of basic writing viewed "conflict and struggle . . . as the enemies of Basic Writing instruction" (890). Lu argues that Shaughnessy and her contemporaries were promising "'effective' ways of appeasing the kind of 'hostility' or 'militancy' feared in open admissions students. The appeal of this line of thinking is that it protects the autonomy of the 'literate community' while also professing a solution to the 'threat' the open admissions students seem to pose to the university" (895). Critical to this notion of acculturating students to the academic niceties and the more "civilized" culture of the university are the assumptions that basic writers are exclusively products of the open-admissions phenomenon and minority students, who are "indifferent to learning" (891). Critical to this notion is the status of the basic writing teacher her/himself in relation to these unwanted, uncivilized basic writing students. Such teachers realized that

> the questionable academic status of not only their students (seen as "ill-prepared") but also themselves (Basic Writing was mostly assigned to beginning teachers, graduate students, women, minorities, and the under-employed but tenured members of other departments) would pressure teachers like Shaughnessy . . . to find legitimacy for their subject. (890)

Lu's study is important to a consideration of basic writing for elite students for two reasons. First, the assumption that the basic writing students whom these teachers encountered were and always *are* underprivileged, minority students who are "indifferent to learning" belies the inclusion of basic writers among the earlier classes of institutions like Harvard that, by their own admission standards, excluded nonwhite students as well as poorly motivated students. In fact, Harvard president James B. Conant declared in 1940 that despite a desperate attempt to fill all eleven hundred incoming freshmen seats, the university still sought to ensure that "no one should be admitted to Harvard College who has not at least a 50/50 chance of being promoted to the sophomore class." Such was an attempt to, in historian Marcia G. Synott's words, "bring in enough paying customers" without visibly "lowering standards" ("Changing 'Harvard Student'" 196). Second, the teachers whom Lu claims to have sought "legitimacy" for basic writing are, in theory, partly to blame for the field's current ignorance regarding basic writing students as they have historically existed at elite institutions. Such institutions are not typically viewed as sites of employment for the marginalized teacher—or the "underemployed"—whom basic writing scholarship generally perceives as the champions of basic writing students. Teachers such as these, as well as the heroic figures whom Gunner analyzes, may only exist in writing program lore, but they are hard to imagine as the faculty of elite institutions—where English department faculty are pictured as literary scholars who are, in Gunner's analysis, "unable to be the kind of `real) teacher that the Basic writing teacher by definition is" (33). This teacher-hero-figure is almost inextricably linked with basic writing advocacy narratives, with the assumption that all basic writers are in need of such extraordinary saviors in order to succeed. Again, there are institutional settings in which such heroic advocacy is necessary and does occur. But Gunner rightly points out that this kind of "iconic discourse" (33) about basic writing teachers only serves to further mythologize how and why basic writing classrooms operate as intellectual islands adrift from the larger university—which valorizes basic writing as a political space antithetical to the loftier and, in the first half of the twentieth century, more "gentlemanly" physical and social setting of the elite institution.

These varied definitions of and responses to the concept of "basic" must now be put to the historical test, especially as they are constructed as post–open admissions and as incompatible with the social and economic conditions at elite institutions. The next chapter examines the prevailing discourse, as published in early issues of composition studies' professional journals and as analyzed in studies of that era, concerning remedial writers and "precollege" students from the 1920s through the 1960s. In doing so, I demonstrate that these ongoing, critical controversies over who basic writers are and where and how they are taught were in place prior to Shaughnessy's work and within institutional locations at all levels of selectivity nationwide.

3

Before 1960: The Rise of the Boneheads

> [L]et me note the most serious of our responsibilities as teachers of English, a responsibility best designated in the phrase: *our duty to stamp out illiteracy*. . . . This arduous, uninteresting, laborious task is the first, the most essential of all our duties as English teachers, I repeat: Stamp out, wipe out, destroy and away with, as far as possible, inability, clumsiness, ineptitude in the ordinary use, in speaking and writing, of our English mother tongue.
>
> —Felix Emanuel Schelling, *Pedagogically Speaking: Essays and Addresses on Topics More or Less Educational*, 1929

> English composition is, without question, one of the most fundamental subjects in our schools. There is no study that so thoroughly permeates the work of all other subjects and that is so successful to their understanding. From one viewpoint every recitation is a language recitation and has to do with English composition work in some way or the other. English composition affords an opportunity by which the student may be able to express his ideas in a logical and grammatical way.
>
> —Anonymous Purdue freshman, 1926

THE EPIGRAPHS, CULLED BY composition studies historians Marolina Salvatori and John Brereton, evidence that clarity and correctness of expression were virtually synonymous with both student and teacher notions of proficient English composition in early twentieth-century America. The need to put primary emphasis on grammar, spelling, and mechanics in first-year student writing—and the loathing that the *need* for such instruction created for English instructors—stemmed from the increasingly mechanized approach to higher education that followed World War I, the influx into the university of middle-class student populations, and the subsequent advent of large-scale composition programs such as those at Stanford and Harvard universities. This early composition program machinery made the ever-present split between instruction in expository writing and instruction in literary analysis and appreciation all the more visible, a split that continues in many visible ways in both high schools and universities today. As Thomas Masters notes, this emphasis on and desire for surface correctness intensified throughout the 1940s and 1950s, resulting in the revival of themes-based courses and large-scale valuations of clean, unadulterated prose. In the university's eyes, only when such cleanliness had been achieved could students be trusted to undertake the complexities of literary work and other higher-order thinking tasks across the curriculum. As the intellectual and ideological location of mainstream, introductory English literary instruction, therefore, rested at the bottom of the educational hierarchy, so-called remedial pedagogies, such as English composition (née rhetoric) resided much further still, in the curricular basement.

The sociointellectual history of composition as an introductory subject has been well documented. The larger political climate for *basic* writing as a kind of subintroductory subject in the United States during the first half of the twentieth century has been less well investigated. A question I wish to pursue here, then, is how this national clamor for proficiency in first-year college composition set the universal tone for what underprepared first-year writers were similarly facing in the Ivy League. Another way of putting this question is to ask: Has location *mattered enough* to the scholars examining the conditions of basic writing and basic writers (then-remedial) during the first half of the twentieth century? A sampling of the type and scope of essay and reports published in *English Journal*, *College English*, and *College Composition and Communication* from the early 1920s through the late 1950s provides some insight into the historical scrutiny put upon basic writing and basic writers during this era as well as the proposed "remedies" for eliminating the need for remedial programs in English. Even if the administrators, or even the English faculty, at Yale and Harvard were not active readers of these field journals, it is evident from the policies and pedagogies enforced at these elite universities that the call-to-arms of the proficiency "crisis" in larger American society did not escape their collective eyes and ears.

As evident in these early publications, early scholarship in composition studies more closely resembled opinion essays or pedagogical summaries ("Here's what I do with *my* remedial students"), as opposed to the more theoretical, deeply researched and intricately cited articles of today's scholarship. Submissions published were brief, usually no more than seven or eight pages, were almost always free of any outside references or citations, and were highly descriptive, sometimes narrative, regarding local teaching or curricular conditions, even as they hoped to generalize (i.e., promote) their local pedagogies to a wider national audience.

Maureen Daly Goggin notes that *College English*, as a "spin-off" of *English Journal*, billed itself as "a scholarly journal, a critical review, a teacher's guide, and a news bulletin for the National Council of Teachers of English" (41). Despite this broad range of interests and features, however, the journal "lacked symmetry under the first three editors [W. Wilbur Hatfield, Frederick L. Gwynn, and James E. Miller,] . . . the longest leg by far being given over to literature" (41). Goggin states that most manuscripts concerning composition were "divert[ed]" to the new journal *College Composition and Communication* once it began publication in 1950. These *CCC* articles, focusing on program design, administrative issues, and other emerging trends in first-year writing curricula, were of a slightly more substantial depth and quality than had been previously printed in *English Journal* or *CE*. But the majority of the pieces that focused on first-year composition or remedial composition in both *CE* and *CCC* were what Goggin calls "testimonial pieces" or those that "portray a phenomenon without argument, interpretation, evaluation, or critique" (45–46). It was not until the mid-1960s that the "testimonial" format dissipated and the more citation-heavy scholarship used currently began to emerge.

Even though, Goggin says, such a format was not exactly compelling reading—citing Ken Macrorie's remark that the "dull" nature of *CCC* caused it to resemble "an auto-parts catalog" (qtd. in Goggin 47)—these early publications now serve a valuable archival function, allowing an unfettered look into various programs and program attitudes and philosophies from a range of institutions and institutional types prior to the more recent, post-Shaughnessy advocacy for an analysis of underprepared college writers. Though issues of these journals provide multiple examples of this historical discussion, I have tried to select a representative few that most succinctly raise key debates and points of argument that continue in today's discussions of basic writing and first-year writing in general.

Three key issues relevant to remedial writing and underprepared writers were beginning to emerge during the 1920s to 1950s. I have selected these issues not only because they organize the types and nature of scholarship being published but also because they are issues that seem to still apply to teaching discussions in the twenty-first century, for right or wrong, and that, therefore, trickle into public discussions of writing as a competency versus a means of learning.

First, institutions in the early twentieth century struggled with the classification of standard first-year writing as a *secondary school* skill set that certain students must "make up" upon entering college, as opposed to viewing such instruction as college work. Even though many pundits today argue that secondary schools are *suddenly* "failing" our children, such criticisms—founded or otherwise—have been in place for the twentieth and twenty-first centuries. Second, institutions between 1920 and 1960 questioned whether separate classes for underprepared writers were better, overall, than "mainstreaming" all writers (though this terminology was not yet in use) and debated where and how to delineate between remedial and "regular" writing students and under what type of faculty guidance. Such questions included debates over how to construct and staff remedial writing courses and how to evaluate remedial writing students.

Finally, institutions struggled with how to integrate underprepared writers into the university at large—specifically, whether to accept them into academic programs or to relegate them to nonacademic centers and/or tutoring systems that supported but did not officially disrupt or alter the regular curriculum. One outcome of this discussion was the movement to eliminate remedial writing programs altogether—as the University of Illinois chose to do in 1960. This act of elimination was replicated in the CUNY system about forty years later. Examining the rhetoric of these discussions allows one to see the frequently disparaging, occasionally paternalistic, and often frustrating attitudes toward underprepared student writers prior to Shaughnessy's work, setting the stage for my in-depth look at remedial instruction at Yale and Harvard during this time period.

BLAME IT ON THE HIGH SCHOOLS

It is clear from literature of the time that far before open admissions, there was a rising need for so-called pre-college courses at the university level, focused on the usual scapegoat: failing secondary-school preparation and/or the lack of continuity between high-school- and college-level instruction. Such arguments permeate the earliest pages of *English Journal* and *College English*, evidencing not just the preoccupation of the public but also that of the field of composition studies, with the disconnections between high-school- and college-level writing instruction.

In 1922's *English Journal*, two articles appeared on the subject of high-school-to-college transitions. George R. Coffman's "Correlation between High School and College English" summarized recent changes in college-admissions procedures and the concomitant changes in the prior view of high school as a "preparatory" site of instruction. Coffman notes the increasing number of colleges using criteria other than the College Board exams to create their entering freshmen classes: "This is a period of readjustment in the educational world" (129). He cites a local satirist writing in an educational journal who imagines, "From now on credit will be given for sweeping the floor, raising poultry, building dog houses . . . and for other home enterprises requiring the intelligence and skill acceptable to the institutions of lower learning" (qtd. in 135). The satirist continues by focusing his ire on English departments: "It has always seemed to me unfair that universities should insist on ability to use good English and an acquaintance with English literature as rigid prerequisites for admission" (qtd. in 135). Coffman considers these skeptical views alongside the realities of shifting admission policies and proclaims, "[U]nder present conditions state higher educational institutions could no longer expect to do much toward educating leaders" (136). In reference to first-year composition, Coffman argues,

> With sub-Freshman classes, secondary school English is being pushed up into our colleges and universities. As a corollary to what we have said above, the danger of this to the general intellectual life of the institution is obvious when we consider that the weakest as well as the strongest student and the sub-Freshman as well as the graduate courses establish the intellectual norm. (136)

In addition to this piece's larger view that high school work is bleeding into college curricula, Coffman's piece also presents an interesting term: the "intellectual norm," without stating what that "norm" is or should be. He states, "Minimum essentials in English composition for unconditioned entrance into the freshman class are becoming pretty generally established," implying later that these standards include "minimum essentials in literature" (136). But the specific criteria creating the demarcation between "Freshman" and "sub-Freshman" are left open. That this norm is "intellectual," as opposed to vocational or practical, propagates the view that under-prepared writers are not just lacking *skills* but also lacking necessary *intelligence*, further locating these student writers somewhere outside of the typical student population, socially separated by their *lack*.

A second related article in the 1922 *English Journal* was "The Prescribed Work in College English: Its Relation to the Secondary Schools," by Helen Sard Hughes, of Wellesley College, who takes a different approach to the subject of so-called make-up work in English composition at the college level. She states openly that

> It is my belief that these two elementary courses [first-year writing and second-year introduction to literature] are for the most part wastefully negative in function. They are given

> chiefly to prevent trouble. They are founded on the supposition (not always easy to disprove) that the high-school training in English is of little value; that the college must lay its own foundations before the student can be trusted to enter upon new and intensive work in English or in any other subject requiring competence in organizing material and stating facts. (200)

Though a view such as this seems, initially, to be progressive—giving the high schools due credit for providing full and helpful instruction in writing—the core of Hughes's complaint is more reactionary and focused on the inadequacies of the college curricula and its students. Hughes strongly resists the notion that colleges (such as Wellesley, whose first-year curriculum she briefly outlines) should "repeat" instruction offered at the high-school level, because any problems that students incur upon writing in the college setting are proof of "*bad habits*, not *bad instruction*" (201) as well as the accelerated pace in which the student must produce work. Hughes recommends for students "in need of further training" a "drill course in organization . . . with a view to the correction of bad habits and confirming of good ones" emphasizing note-taking, bibliography basics, and source usage (202). She argues that the present course in "amateur sociology, economics, politics, education, and what not, offered in the guise of English composition, is making the English teacher a charlatan and his pupils glib jugglers with the half-understood facts and phrases which feed their passion for superficial survey, and take the edge of novelty from the more earnest investigation of these subjects" (203).

Of course, one can hear echoes of what Berlin coined the "current-traditionalist" argument against subject-based, critical pedagogy–centered course designs embedded in Hughes's complaints, as well as the skeptical review of today's composition curricula by public and nonacademic observers who question why engaging students in *subject matter*—sometimes of any kind—is more beneficial (or should take "time" away from) critical instruction in spelling, grammar, usage, and citation methods. Importantly, Hughes questions the general *need* for the presence of first-year composition in the colleges at all—a question also continued today in discussions of how to "streamline" the path toward a student's degree, and offered as an alternative to students who hope to "test out" of first-year writing, Such a conception of the college writing course necessitates seeing it as *repetitive* rather than *new* intellectual work, a critical impediment to understanding the formation of composition studies as not only a subject but also a distinct scholarly discipline. Such a conception also puts higher value on the population of students who were waived or exempted from the required course or sequence as the target, ideal demographic on the college campus.

This foundational problem of seeing first-year composition as a "real" course rather than a repetitive requirement serving neither students nor faculty was an important building block in the finger-pointing that occurred regarding the so-called Sub-Freshman in first-year college writing. As Alvin Fountain argues regarding "The Poorly Prepared Student" in the January 1940 issue of *College English*, institutions that ask, "Why is it necessary for some of the best universities in the country . . . to give this special work below college level?" can look to high-school teachers who are "overloaded in students and in hours" and who "labor under [the] handicaps" brought upon by large classes, wherein there is no time to read and discuss student writing (317). Further complicating the less-than-ideal conditions of teaching at the secondary level was the concern that there was a lack of continuity between high school and college curricula. Robert C. Pooley said, "It is easy to make accusations; to assail the high schools for not doing their duty or to bemoan the poor quality of modern college students," but encouraged his readers to assume instead that "high-school teachers by and large want to do their full duty and are working faithfully at it" (149).

Pooley acknowledges two important realities for secondary schools, realities still with us today: first, that "the range of ability in many high school classes is enormous" and. second, that "high school teachers are not generally well-enough informed as to the standards of composition demanded by college courses" as they "tended to pass through Freshman English" without a struggle (150). In addition, Pooley reminds his audience that the purpose of the first-year English course is somewhat unclear: "Is [it] to be regarded merely as necessary, but grudged, make-up? It is designed to do what the high school failed to do—to make good writers of all freshmen? . . . Let us view this matter realistically. Can we as college teachers set up a clear definition of what we mean by ability to write English on the college level?" (152). Pooley concludes his article by offering a few criteria for entering freshmen—including their ability to write work that is "reasonably free from mechanical defects" and to have read "a number of books with intelligent grasp of their contents" (153). He also recommends that colleges and high schools form articulation committees and that college instructors visit high schools regularly to "learn rather than to teach" in those settings (153–54).

Pooley's piece could have been written today; each of his questions and queries is still alive in the debate over preparation from high school to college. Additionally, the points he raises impact upon not only how we define "standard" English composition goals at the first-year level but how, in turn, we determine the goals of "remedial" composition. Pooley rightly questions what role the high schools *should* play in this debate, strongly implying that it is impossible to serve all students equally well or to ensure total preparedness for college writing, given the conditions present in the secondary classroom. Pooley also asks where English composition should be located, physically and pedagogically speaking. If the high-school teacher is not able to reasonably instruct students in expository writing, then is it, in fact, appropriate for the college instructor instead to take up this instruction?

A comparative view is offered in Theodore J. Gates's essay "The First Instruction in Composition" from *College English* (1941). Though its title sounds like a historical look at the field of first-year writing, Gates's use of the term *first* is meant to indicate where to *start* in the first-year writing classroom—what to "teach first" (64). Gates comments on the first page of his piece, "[T]here is no downward limit to the curriculum which you *may* find it necessary to devise. Happy is the teacher and university who has no student needing instruction on the lower levels" (64), yet on the next page he says, "Still another count to prove that we cannot wash our hands of a dirty job is the increased number of colleges and universities which have established various kinds of remedial courses—sub-freshman courses—some carrying whole or partial credit and some carrying none. The amount of credit usually depends upon what the traffic will bear. . . . [T]he high schools and [secondary] academies are determining our curriculums for these students. . . . Fortunately, there is an upper quarter or an upper half to which training of a collegiate rank can be offered. For these we are grateful; they save our sanity and our lives" (65). In response to this divergent group of incoming students, Gates offers three proposals: first, that secondary schools "discourage the several brands of 'vocational' English" offered; second, that college teachers "fight the overloading" of high school faculty; and third, that "the high school teacher who does have time to teach" concentrate "her efforts toward the development of two essential skills in her students," namely reading well and writing "clearly and without subsequent embarrassment" (67).

Gates's essay is an important archival document of midcentury attitudes toward not only high school curricula and academic organization but also the distaste that underprepared students were met with once arriving at college, despite that college teachers were beginning to recognize that these students were underprepared through no particular, innate fault of their own but instead through the mismanagement and overloading of their previous writing teachers. Gates's disdain for the "dirty job" that is remedial instruction is at odds with his later sympathies for the setting in which these students were taught; yet, he later comments that colleges also contribute to the presence of these students—that they have been "too willing to accept as worthy and approved candidates all and sundry who have had the necessary fee in hand" (68). In other words, it is not just the fault of the high schools but also the colleges that underprepared students exist.

Finally, as a more progressive example of the reality of high-school-to-college connections, collaborations, and failures, Robert J. Cadigan in "The Private Secondary School and the College" in the May 1942 issue of *College English* acknowledges, "There is at present such a lack of uniformity among the high-school and college teachers that it is almost impossible to generalize from specific experiences or observations" (735). He argues that there are many students who, even though advised against college due to poor high school performance, enroll in a "reputable institution, frequently the one of his choice" and faces a struggle upon arrival. . . . Whether [this student's] academic career terminates in January or in June of his first year depends not so much upon the boy as upon the nature of the preconceived standards of the institution" (736–37). Cadigan also describes other student types, such as the gifted but lazy student and the "faithful worker" student. He attributes this variety of student types not only to the variability of the general population but also to the variability of the types of teachers and preferred pedagogies to which each of these students gravitates. While all teachers have in common being "tired," they "share a great many hopes for these students as they send them on to college" (741).

Cadigan's article ultimately shifts the responsibility for accommodating students onto the *college*, arguing that if institutions are going to accept students with diverse learning needs, they need to find a way to help them, calling to "Come unto us, all ye who are oppressed with spelling and misplaced modifiers" (737). Cadigan wants all incoming students to "find some provision for individual differences, [and] not all be stretched on the Procrustean bed of arbitrary standards" (741). As such, Cadigan is making a subtle argument for layered levels within the writing curriculum—basic, standard, advanced—without saying so outright. He is also arguing that it does no real good to blame the teachers, the high school, or the students *themselves* so long as colleges readily accept students of all preparedness and, in effect, promise them an education regardless. Cadigan's view previews more recent basic writing scholarship that argues for access and accessibility among diverse student populations and celebrates the unique literacies of each incoming freshman. In addition, by invoking private high schools in his argument, Cadigan introduces the possibility for advocacy for underprepared (or undermotivated) students who graduate from a more elite setting, which interestingly complicates the notion that it is the *public* (read: inner-city, urban, minority) secondary schools that produce all or the vast majority of underprepared college writers.

DESIGNING A COURSE, DEFINING A STUDENT: METHODOLOGIES

Such concerns about accommodating underprepared writers are evidenced in other institutions' responses to their growing need for separate remedial writing courses and their own changing enrollment and admissions trends during the 1930s through the 1950s. Colleges and universities were coming to recognize that the catch-all "Freshman English" course—partially due to the diverse abilities of the student body but also due to the inability to accurately predict how well any given student's high-school instruction would align with the values of the postsecondary institution—did not adequately serve the needs of all first-year writers. Consequently, institutions were creating "remedial" courses without a clear sense of how to construct this curriculum or how to evaluate whether such courses allowed students to gain the specifically local definition of "proficiency" required by each institution.

As noted in "A National Survey of Conditions of Freshman English" (1929), the desire to "classify" students based on level of preparation in academic writing was widespread as early as the late 1920s. The survey's author, Warner Taylor of the University of Wisconsin, argued,

> There is a strong growing tendency in the country to assign students to such divisions of Freshman English as will be most suited to their training and capacity. The argument I have heard most often against the practice contends that the draining off of talent from a class leaves a dead-level sediment difficult of stirring up emotionally and mentally; that bright students serve to stimulate dull. But pedagogically the 'ayes' seem to have it: Well prepared and intelligent Freshmen can advance faster and master a more exacting program with greater profit to themselves. (qtd. in Brereton 554)

The argument that it is better to separate the "dull" students, ultimately, in favor of helping the 'bright" ones is part of the powerful machinery of basic writing that has historically justified the separation of such students in the classroom—not to provide *extra* help for basic writers or to recognize their particular learning needs but to keep them *away* from the mainstream, to avoid doing harm to the massive middle. Many basic writing scholars today continue to advocate for well-designed and separate basic writing courses as located on equal footing within the curriculum—those with small caps, extensive one-on-one work, and a positive learning atmosphere that emphasizes intellectual growth. Such separation, however, was not always so positive—and was sometimes motivated by the need to keep the "good" students away from the "bad." Such physical and intellectual separation was—and is—often the consequence of separating out the "bright" students into Honors classes or advanced tracks, so that they might learn on their own, unfettered by more "average" colleagues. Of the 232 institutions responding to Taylor's 1929 survey, 30 schools, or 14 percent, offered a "sub"freshman course; comparatively, 24 schools, or 11 percent, offered an "advanced" course beyond freshman English. Those offering *both* "sub" and "advanced" courses numbered 56, or 26 percent of respondents. Taylor notes that these institutions responding had 500 or more students enrolled (qtd. in Brereton 555).

Two interesting pieces from *English Journal* outline specific remedial programs at Syracuse University and the University of Texas, programs designed to employ the separate-and-classify approach to assisting underprepared writers. Norman J. Whitney, in "Ability Grouping at Syracuse" (1924), uses a forward-sounding, and ultimately forward-thinking, term to describe this institution's local approach to classifying underprepared students. Whitney makes clear that his article is an apolitical one, as it "is not [his] purpose to discuss the advantages of sectioning classes on the basis of ability" but instead to simply describe Syracuse's course plan (482). Notable among Whitney's points about the course is its initiative to group students not just as "ready" or "not ready" for Syracuse's first-year writing course but to group students through the use of the "Minimum Essentials Test," consisting of one section on grammar and another requiring a theme (483). The testing also allowed for "misfits and mistakes" (483) that made provisions for later promotion as well as demotion to the appropriate level writing course. In doing so,

Whitney asserts, Syracuse avoided the "objectionable classification 'sub-Freshmen'" (484). Consequently, "there is no stigma attached to the lowest group; credit is given for the work in the usual manner. . . . [O]nly the more fortunate are exempt from the regular requirement. We reward the better students in proportion to their deserving; there is no penalty for the poorer" (484).

Such a placement system, which emphasizes *exemption* (or proficiency) rather than *failure* in its design, certainly avoids the stigma of a remedial designation, at least on the surface, and thus stands out in its curricular thinking. Still, this ability grouping—into groups A, B, and C—resulted in the "first semester [course] required of Group C students" only being "largely a course in sentences," although the goal had been to find students to be "free of the structural errors which embarrass [those] who have not had this training" (Whitney 487). As such, the developmental, first-semester course was generally devoid of *actual* writing, as still tends to be the case in many noncredit basic writing courses today.

A contrasting example of a course-placement system is the one at the University of Texas, described in David Lee Clark's 1929 *English Journal* essay "Classification of Freshmen." The article focuses also on three ability groupings, classified based on results of a two-part exam as "those who pass both creditably; those who pass one and fail the other . . . the 'doubtful' group; and those who fail both. Students in the last group are put at once in Zero English" (330). Approximately 13 percent, or 139 students, fell into the third category of double failure and were placed into English Zero or "OA" (330, 333). The majority of this article is an enumeration of the placement results and a reprinting of the exam itself, typical of other articles (or elements thereof) published in this time. However, Clark notes that one part of the piece—"the method of selection for the Zero course"—is "given in detail to show that the committee is after all quite lenient" (330). Nonetheless, placement *at once* into this course was demanded—without wasting a moment that could be spent acculturating students in writing.

As such courses came to occupy a position in first-year writing curricula, a wave of not only descriptive program narratives but also more general how-to essays began to appear. Some of these essays discussed remedial writing—or general underpreparedness—not by outlining a specific course, placement process, or overall program but by delineating the benefits and drawbacks of standard composition courses. H. Bunker Wright's "What Freshman Composition Cannot Do" in *College English* (1945) set forth clear reasons for substandard writing. Bunker contends, "If every instructor insists on good writing and speaking and if he shows his disapproval of careless composition, he will make the pleasant discovery that much of the poor English of which he has complained is due to the students' indifference and indolence rather than inability or ineffective training" (101). Consequently, all that a teacher need do is "call [errors] to the attention of the perpetrators and brand them as serious blemishes," whereupon they will cease to occur (101). While Wright recognizes that there are limitations to the composition course—such as staffing shortages and an overwhelming number of students enrolled—he believes that "what is needed is not a new plan; it is a new attitude" on the part of instructors (99). Even though he admits that poorly trained students do exist in composition courses, he assures readers that with the proper attitude and attention to "eradicat[ing] old habits" (100), students' writing will improve. Wright does not lay claim to such improvement *lasting* over the next four years but seems to take pride in insisting that for the *short-term*, there is no reason why writing teachers cannot give their "students a necessary discipline" that they will then take into their upper-division courses across the curriculum (101).

While Wright's essay sounds more like a pep-rally speech than an academic essay, it lays the groundwork for what composition studies professionals still argue: the job is *not* to teach student writers *everything* they need to know but to introduce literacy-based strategies in order that the students might apply these strategies, both inside and outside of the classroom, after the writing courses end. However, Wright is perhaps overly confident in the idea that *all* writing evidencing structural problems or difficulty can be cured by simple discipline and that no writer is truly insufficiently trained. But his view was apparently shared by other faculty and administrators who sought to shock or humiliate students into writing better—and in doing so reduce the "burden" of remedial writing instruction.

One such perspective is provided by Milton Milhauser in "Universal English at the University of Bridgeport" in a 1949 issue of *College English.* Milhauser briefly outlines the course curricula and general philosophy for the universal English program at this Connecticut private college. Milhauser's overview includes faculty directives relevant to subpar work in writing:

> Under the universal English program, all members of the faculty have been directed to refuse written work which does not meet prescribed minimum standards of expression. Unsatisfactory papers are not penalized in grade; they are simply refused. Nor are deficiencies in expression indicated. The burden is placed squarely where it belongs—on the student. He must re-write the paper, which is first accepted for grading when it is submitted in amended form. He is thus realistically penalized for doing a job badly—by having to do it twice. Almost inevitably, he incurs a further penalty for late submission of work; but it is a matter of indifference to the program whether he is penalized at all. What matters is that he has been forced to apply what he has learned. (340)

Such all-or-nothing rhetoric significantly echoes Felix Emanuel Schelling's call to "stamp out illiteracy," given in this chapter's first epigraph. The University of Bridgeport's plan to assist underprepared writers is, in fact, not a plan of *assistance* at all: it is a plan that seeks to ritualize the writing process so that students, like well-trained dogs, will "learn" not to make errors or face penalty and humiliation (and fail to receive even the reading time of their instructor/s). Bridgeport's methodologies are self-described as "precise, stringent, and minute" in nature, in response to "industry and graduate school" demand for improvement in student writing (340). This system encourages basic writers to lament their location within the university and lack of status and be thus motivated to magically change it to avoid further embarrassment and highlighting of their innate failures.

This pedagogy of *refusal*—rather than consideration or accommodation—was limited to the unnamed but implied "regular" first-year writing course in the program. Milhauser notes that "seriously deficient students may be required to take additional formal courses in composition as a prerequisite for graduation" (341), though there is no mention made of how such students are determined to be in need of this course or how many "refusals" constitute a need for this additional coursework. Ultimately, Milhauser says that the faculty have accepted this universal English program, albeit for selfish reasons because the program "involves no 'red tape' and a minimum of administrative interference in the classroom . . . and it eases the instructor's burden. He is given no additional task to perform, and he is permitted to refuse to read an obscure, illiterate, illegible, or simply slovenly paper" (341). Again, no mention is made of the concomitant "burden" put upon instructors for the remedial or "additional formal courses" in composition.

As a rare and contrasting approach to instructing remedial writers, "This Game of Writing: A Study in Remedial English," by Carrie Ellen Stanley and published in 1943 in *College English*, outlines a more flexible, personally tailored plan that seeks to raise students up rather than humiliate them downward.[1] Such an approach is perhaps the ancestor to the modern notion of reading "supportively" when evaluating student writing, particularly that which is connected to placement or intake measurements. Stanley's essay was part of a genre of how-to pieces designed to provide local, well-intentioned, perspectives into the remedial writing course or its implementation on the local campus. Stanley's title comes from an extended narrative at the start of her essay describing an unnamed freshman remedial writing student who was also a star basketball player at her institution, Iowa State University. Stanley's essay focuses on how to engage a variety of students in this course located, in her words, in the "outer fringes of composition" (424). She offers the description for the course, from its initial announcement in the university bulletin. Iowa State's Remedial English "laboratory" was designed

> to provide opportunity for directed practice in composition for those who write under continued handicaps. . . . [I]nstruction

> is open to students who are recommended by any instructor as deficient in, or hampered by, even slight particulars of composition. Remedial English offers no credit; it yields no grade; it has no requirement other than a spirit of willingness on the part of the student, whose agreement to appear is wholly voluntary; it is, in fact, not a course at all. To improve his ability in evaluating his ideas and his skill in presenting them will be a student's only purpose in seeking the assistance offered. (424)

To the modern ear, this description sounds very much like the structure of a small writing *center*, especially as the language emphasizes that Remedial English is "not a course at all." In this way, Stanley's approach is a quasi-positive spin on *location*, as it marks separation vis-à-vis support rather than punishment or quarantine. Yet, at this point in the institution's history, at least, the "laboratory" concept still had a course-like label and was regulated by instructor perceptions of student deficiencies. Stanley states that "no one who asks for it is refused a place" (424), but it seems doubtful that any student was *choosing* to be associated with Remedial English, despite her enthusiastic portrayal of the academic makeovers such a course location offered. At the conclusion of her essay, Stanley relates the aforementioned student athlete's transformation from a "Fd" (failure) student to a "B" student: "Truly not a miracle. . . . Put on his own, a young man may grow up!" (428).

So is imbedded another thread present in early publications on remedial writing instruction: a somewhat paternalistic attitude toward these writers who were implicitly or explicitly characterized as less-developed *in general* or less mature than other, better-prepared students of the time. Such an attitude prevails on some campuses today, where basic writers are often described as lacking the maturity to be integrated into the "regular" curriculum, particularly in the case of minority student groups. Susie McD. W. Rabourn, in her 1931 *English Journal* piece, "English Curriculum for Pupils of Low I.Q.," similarly warns that "slow group" writing students are "restless, impulsive, and sometimes inclined to be disorderly" (449). As a result, Rabourn cautions teachers to teach "these pupils . . . self-restraint. As someone has expressed it, 'self-repression instead of self-expression,'" and that these writers need a "quiet, peaceful atmosphere to serve as anodyne for their restlessness and excitability" (450). Such rhetoric recalls Min-Zhan's Lu argument that a lack of *control* in overall *social behavior* is how basic writers are often characterized.[2]

Stanley also subtly invokes the call of patriotism into this maturity equation, stating that the remedial student writer eventually "can express what he wishes to express and understand what he needs to understand from the words of others. This is a freedom that armies today are defending" (428). Such an invocation, I believe, is no accident, given the wartime publication date of her essay and the anticipated numbers of returning soldiers who would be shuttled into remedial-style writing courses after World War II, which would create debates over how to accommodate yet another type of student writer.

Thomas Masters, in his book *Practicing Writing: The Postwar Discourse of Freshman English,* claims that campuses indeed "struggled to deal with the new ethical and ideological framework of post-World War II America" (13). Masters indicates that Wheaton College's Army Specialized Training Program included returning GIs who were "matured by travel and peril, by tough discipline, and by their awareness of the value of an education" (13). In addition to articles on the overall remedial writing student population, several brief articles during the mid-1940s were also focused on how to accommodate the nontraditional or "special" remedial student, in this context the returning soldier. Such discussion was in relation to the Army Specialized Training Program, foisted on American colleges and universities during World War II.

One such article was Gilbert L. Bond's 1946 *College English* piece, "A Postwar Program for the Remedial-Student," which cautioned that although remedial English courses had been labeled "dummy English" or "hospital English," faculty should note that the returning soldier who seeks remedial work "is nearly always appreciative of and grateful for any sincere effort to help him" (469). Bond says that even though "the remedial-English student will be with us for some time to come, [so] we may just as well accept him" (466), a remedial program "does not preclude the maintenance of necessary high standards. . . . [R]ather, it represents a conscious attempt to help the deserving student instead of leaving him entirely to the old battle of the survival of the fittest" (469). Following this line of thinking, Bond suggests that universities allow remedial courses to "satisfy the requirements for English composition upon successful completion, but make it clear that the student will be remanded to the course *at any time* . . . upon the recommendation of the instructor" (468, emphasis added).

Most fascinating about Bond's piece is his use of medically based terminology to label basic writers—perhaps the earliest precursor of negative connotations for basic writing as terminally flawed. Mike Rose relates that in the 1930s, remedial courses were labeled "sick sections" and in the following decade, "hospital sections," partially due to the origins of the term *remedial* in medical terminology focusing on mentally deficient students ("Language of Exclusion" 352). At Harvard, the doctor-patient relationship between teacher and student also pervaded the terminology of first-year writing, as students were required to complete their "prescription" of required English composition and if unsuccessful in the standard course of English A, were thereafter "prescribed" additional coursework in writing.

But Bond's piece, despite its medically based rhetoric, is also noteworthy for its contradictions in terms; he is advocating, at once, a small class size, skilled instructor, and careful planning of reading and writing assignments for the remedial English course, while suggesting that this rubber-band proposition is always in effect regardless; a student could be snapped back into the course at any time, based on an instructor's judgment, and, therefore, was never potentially "free" of the stigma of remediation. Bond seems to genuinely want to assist underprepared students, but his argument is careful to position the university as a place of "standards," rather than reactive accommodations. He resigns himself to the notion that such students "will be with us for some time" to reinforce that this is not a temporary trend; this observation, however, is surely more defeatist than welcoming.

INCLUSION OR EXCLUSION: WHITHER BASIC WRITING?

As the 1950s began, many universities began experimenting with overall curricular revision, including the advent of "General Education" course work at Harvard and other institutions. An allied result of this revision was the reconsideration of remedial courses and their position in the institution—specifically, whether the inclusion of such courses should entail accompanying penalties or disincentives to the students enrolled. In particular, debates began over the literal location of composition—turning to not only the community (a.k.a. "junior") colleges but also distinct offices and centers within the four-year campus—to resituate remedial writing and remedial writers. Kenneth E. Eble's 1957 essay, "What Happened to the Boneheads?" is typical of the institutional response to surges in basic writing enrollments during this time. Eble laments the continued presence of "boneheads," the disparaging nickname for remedial writing students at his institution: "The University of Utah, like many other universities, has had remedial English for as long as our senior staff can remember," but only in the early 1950s did it emerge as "a really sizable and troubling enterprise" (2). Yet, Eble happily notes that in the mid-1950s, the boneheads diminished due to the requirement of an additional fee for remedial English course, called English AX, and because all remedial courses—including the lower-level English BX—have been moved from the English department to the "Extension" office at Utah (2–3). Similar strategies are noted in a 1960 *CCC* article about a nationwide survey of remedial English programs. Eight of the seventy-five schools responding charged fees of $10.25 to $36.00 per term for registration in remedial courses, with thirty-five more institutions planning to charge similar fees beginning in September 1961 (Cox, Canario, and Cypher 241).

These institutional strategies to marginalize basic writers—either through financial disincentives and/or through physical segregation of the learning space(s)—are present in universities today that relegate their preparatory writing curriculum to allied community-college locations sponsored or co-opted by the four-year institution or to "skills" centers on the universities' own campuses—thus gaining financially from basic-writing students, not by charging extra fees but by denying *academic credit* for course tuition paid. Such decentering and financial penalization of basic writers are responses to the perceived drain of financial and human resources caused by staffing these courses and attending to these students' needs and are deterrents to students who cannot afford to pay such penalties. Some institutions have even collected all "remedial" programs in one location, regardless of subject matter. In doing so, these campuses link basic writing to instruction in other "deficient" subject matter and by shuttling these programs to a virtually invisible location, marginalize them as distinct from "regular" student learning and the socialization that accompanies it.

Eble's closing reinforces this segregationist impulse: "The number of hopeless students has probably decreased, though the multiple repeater problem is still with us. . . . What has happened to the boneheads shows us once again that college problems, if faced, can be solved by other means than that of making them part of the curriculum" (3). Eble's unabashed use of the term *bonehead* further emphasizes this marginalization and the desire for "regular" students (and faculty) to be separated from such unwashed masses of writers.

This institutional arrangement may be seen as a simple risk-benefit model, one that not all institutions during this period were willing to undertake. The 1957 *CCC* symposium "Has English Zero Seen Its Day?" puts forward two conclusions about the state of remedial writing in the 1950s so far: "No institution which has not offered English Zero plans to introduce it, and the potential English Zero freshman who finds college doors gradually closing against him will assuredly enroll somewhere—but where?" (78). These chilling conclusions imply an unwillingness on the part of colleges and universities during this time period to take significant "risks" on basic writers.

As an example within this 1957 symposium of an elite university's response to the "problem" of remedial writing courses, F. E. Bowman explains Duke University's curriculum:

> For over ten years Duke University has offered English L, a full-credit, three-hour course as a third semester of English composition required of low-ranking entering Freshman. . . .

> Continuing study will attempt to identify entering freshmen who are good enough risks to merit the cost and time of English L instruction. (qtd. in "Has English Zero" 76)

Compare that statement of risk-benefit at a private university to the response from Warner G. Rice, representing a *public* university, the University of Michigan:

> The University of Michigan is in the fortunate position of being able to select its students from the top third of graduates from Michigan high schools, and to exercise a similar selectivity with respect to out-of-state students. Accordingly, we have not found it necessary to offer sub-freshman courses in composition, nor have we any intention of doing so. About ten percent of our freshmen are put in special sections on the basis of their proved ability, and I hope that our distinctions can continue to be between the best and the good, rather than between the good and the poor. (qtd. in "Has English Zero" 81)

And, finally, the somewhat evasive (and rhetorically creative) response from Pooley at the University of Wisconsin–Madison:

> The manifesto from the University of Illinois [eliminating remedial writing programs] has not up to the present affected our policies and plans in Freshman English. After initial testing each fall we *refuse to accept* into the standard freshman English course a certain number of students, usually less than 2% of the freshman class. ("Has English Zero" 94, emphasis added)

Obviously, stratified terms—and pejorative classifications—abound in these exchanges. For Duke, because there is a careful balancing of students who are "good enough" to admit under these conditional grounds and with the assertion that "continuing study" will be done, the university has not decided to permanently offer remedial courses. Duke's explanation, however, is progressive when compared with Michigan's stance, distinguishing between "the best and the good" instead of the "good and the poor."

The comment about Michigan's writing program emphasizes its ability to "select" the best students, implying that it has the freedom to *choose* whether basic writers enter the university, and it simply chooses not to do so. Ironically, the University of Michigan would later host a site for first-year (and basic) writing, the English Composition Board/Sweetland Writing Center. Wisconsin's reply, however, is perhaps the most interesting of the three, as it puts the issue of basic writing curricula not at the level of institutional *admission* but at the level of *course* entrance. Pooley states that the university "refuses to accept" underprepared writers into its regular first-year course; such "refusal" is a fascinating way to translate issues of access. Keep in mind that this is the same Robert Pooley who in the mid-1940s encouraged secondary schools to form articulation committees in partnerships with colleges and similarly encouraged college teachers to be aware of the limitations put upon secondary-school instruction. For the University of Wisconsin, at least as Pooley frames it, the issue appears to have been a true gatekeeping one; students could be "refused" a ticket of admission into the regular/standard writing course, with the alternate path left unstated. This sleight-of-hand keeps Pooley from stating *how* basic writers are accommodated by shifting the focus away from the writers themselves and onto the regular course and who has the right to enter it. Such a response shows how one faculty member's view of remedial writing student accommodation drastically shifted during this era, in just a little over ten years' time.

The next chapter takes a closer look at Yale's approach to basic writing during this period and the school's own interpretation of rights of "refusal" where first year student writers were concerned, reveals some potential responses to these questions of access and integration into not only the English studies curriculum but also the larger university structure. These responses, drawn from archival materials from across the university's historical holdings, obviously are open to change over time. Yet perceptions of location-based valuations of writing instruction still remain rooted in local, institutional values of intellectual pursuit and the vision of the ideal, target student—the "Yale Man."

4

The "Awkward Squad" and Basic Writing at Yale

USING ARCHIVAL DOCUMENTS TO reconstruct the curricular history of a program, let alone an institution's overall view of or attitude toward that program, is not without its hazards. As Patricia Donahue notes, "History is not a scene of objective enactment, but a textual phenomenon, consisting of unstable signifiers to which numerous and equally unstable signifieds can and have been assigned" (222). The materials uncovered in these next two chapters are "unstable" documents that may mean more in certain contexts than in others. Were my project on the primacy of literary instruction at Yale and Harvard, for example, these documents would "mean" quite differently—particularly in the case of Yale, wherein literary instruction came to be infused in first-year writing to the extent that "pure" argumentation and rhetorical training came to signify remediation. Or, were I to make the argument that Yale and Harvard led the way in redefining the modern English department in America, these archival documents might serve as support of the diverse ways in which first-year writing rests at the secure bottom of that department, supporting literature surveys and seminars that float at the top while still holding a strong standard for "correctness" as a foundation for that critical, uniquely aesthetic literary enterprise.

Nevertheless, Donahue's notion that history is a "textual phenomenon" remains a driving force in my study of Yale and Harvard—since without these key memos, policy statements, reports, and even visual renderings, the history of remedial writing at these institutions has so far only existed in the long shadow of "standard" first-year writing, particularly at Harvard, via English A. Donahue herself states, "To say that a beginning serves as a point of demarcation is not to say that it emerges *ex nihilo*, because a beginning can only exist (to the extent that it has any existence at all) as a response to what came before it" (224). Certainly, the work I present here has not sprung fully formed; it is evidence that continues from points at which other scholars left off or turned in a different methodological direction. The histories of Harvard's and, to a lesser extent, Yale's English departments have accumulated their own textual legacies in the research and publications of the field and in the popular press, often further cementing the argument that elite institutions are somehow immune to the problems with student preparedness plaguing other types of universities. Long overdue, therefore, is an investigation into the lesser-known histories of remedial writing at these institutions in order to protest against the assumptions we make when we "locate" basic writing in too narrow a fashion, whether that location is pinpointed via the archives or other types of textual evidence.

This chapter explores the history of Yale's "Awkward Squad" as noted in archival materials and in contemporary, published discussions of Yale's curriculum from approximately 1920 through the late 1950s. The squad's work is examined as both progressive and conservative, sometimes simultaneously, and as a reflection of the lack of importance that Yale placed on writing for "writing's sake" in its curriculum, as John Wozniak relates. The Awkward Squad, born of a misguided, highly conservative attitude toward the value of rhetoric and composition studies in the college curriculum, serves as an early model of remedial writing instruction as shaped by a competitive, elite, and homogeneous educational institution.

HISTORICAL CONDITIONS: YALE AND ECONOMIC FEASIBILITY

Despite the common perception that basic writers have existed only at less-selective institutions of either public or private status, the Ivy League has a long and complicated history of serving particular, institutionally defined versions of underprepared writers. Wozniak's *English Composition in Eastern Colleges 1850–1940* offers data on the prevalence and scope of standard first-year as well as remedial writing in Ivy League and other eastern institutions prior to World War II. His study provides a comprehensive, summative look at the development of composition and rhetoric during these early years of the discipline in American colleges; in addition, his study delineates how the Ivy League stood divided on the issue of where writing courses belonged, particularly in relation to literary study, in the first year and beyond. Wozniak describes this divide as it emerged among Ivy League institutions during the decade of the 1920s:

> [A] more pronounced opposition to compulsory composition in the colleges emanated from influential Yale as well as from Princeton. The long subordination of composition and rhetoric to reading and literature at Yale [resulted in] two camps [that were] definitely arrayed against each other. The one gathered around the standard of Yale and Princeton favored wide reading, literary composition, no formal rhetoric, and only electives for the select few; the other, rallied around the banner of Harvard and Columbia, favored copious writing, logical composition, some rhetoric, and a compulsory course for all, with electives for the many. (139)

Wozniak states that the more conservative institutions, led by Yale, held strong to the belief that writing study as a subject was not of primary importance in the curriculum. James Berlin similarly argues that Yale and Princeton "looked upon the university as the preparatory site for an elite, aristocratic group of individuals [who were to be] immersed in the traditional learning of literature, language and art" rather than professional or vocational training (*Rhetoric and Reality* 71–72). The elective system, Berlin argues, upheld this ideal of "cultivat[ing] the exceptional students" rather than uniformly educating the masses (*Rhetoric and Reality* 71–72). Yale clung to such beliefs throughout the mid-twentieth century, despite that "[e]ven with a smaller, more highly selected student body, teachers [in the Ivy League] had to contend with many students who were poorly prepared. Further, there were never enough teachers nor did they have enough time for the crushing burden of theme correction" (Wozniak 207). Thus, Yale's curriculum may have continued to privilege and prioritize the elite, but it increasingly had to accept and accommodate the non-elite students it was compelled, starting in the 1910s, to admit. In order to keep its desired curriculum intact, Yale chose to create sites of remedial instruction that existed "off the books" rather than bow to the more progressive (and practical) composition curricula found at sister Ivy institutions, such as Harvard.

According to Wozniak's charting of remedial English at twenty-seven private eastern universities (including all eight Ivies), only Dartmouth, Princeton, and Harvard offered courses in remedial writing or writing tutorials during the period 1920 to 1940. Brown, Columbia, Cornell, Penn, and Yale are not credited with offering any remedial writing instruction whatsoever, despite Wozniak's observation of the 1939–40 *Yale Bulletin*'s caution that "evidence that any student is deficient in his command of English will lead to his being required to correct this deficiency by special work" (197). His aggregate data, though extremely thorough and of high historical value, seem incomplete when set against my own archival research. Even though Wozniak's tables do not show any remedial course offerings at Yale, the university did, indeed, have a course that began in the late 1910s, the "Awkward Squad." This course has a complex and somewhat buried history—one worth recovering as an example of the unusual position occupied by basic writing in the Ivy League.

In the early years of the twentieth century, the face of the first-year program was changing nationwide, evolving to meet the needs of the student—and the financial solvency of the institution. The societal function of a college degree, as many other scholars have observed, was also rapidly evolving. To briefly review as an entrée into a discussion of Yale's remedial instruction in this context, we must recall that a great shift in higher education from a selective to a mass-culture pursuit occurred between 1915 and 1940. In 1913, "fewer than one in twenty young persons attended college, and even the most prestigious universities were scrambling to fill their classes" (Levine 16–17). In contrast, by the 1920s, enrollments were rapidly on the rise, reflecting how higher education had "moved into the mainstream of American economic, social, and cultural life" and how universities now "set out to train, accredit, and impart social status to their students" (Levine 17, 19). Berlin points out that in the school year 1919–20, 597,880 students were enrolled in college; by the school year 1929–30, there were 1,100,737; and by 1939–40, 1,494,203 (*Rhetoric and Reality* 58). This rise in enrollment resulted in a greater diversity in the student population, David Russell contends, as "previously excluded social groups were admitted, destroying linguistic homogeneity" (21). However, Russell also argues that such diversity caused the teaching of writing to be an enterprise in "initiating the neophytes into a discourse community" that attempted to re-create the previous, allied community that "shared common values . . . and were then duly welcomed as full members of the nation's governing elite" (20–21).

Thus, through increased shifts would seemingly be good financial news for elite institutions—those in the position to grant social status through the prestige of their degrees and eager to draw qualified applicants from this larger pool—the consequences of college-enrollment trends on the Ivy League were in practice far more complicated and less positive than such data might at first seem to imply. George W. Pierson in his two-volume history of Yale, states that beginning in 1919, the university felt pressured to alter its admission requirements, the first of many accommodations made to allow for greater enrollments beyond the eastern seaboard. In 1916, Jerome Karabel notes, only 12 percent of enrolled Yale men were from west of the Mississippi River (57).

This changing nature of college pursuits forced Yale to reconsider its historical view of admissions in order to stay competitive in a new educational marketplace. As Albert Kitzhaber has shown, Yale College promoted a conservative curriculum in the nineteenth century, one rooted in stubborn tradition and arcane educational values. Yale had been resistant to change—particularly to the German university system, the infrastructure of research, seminars, and graduate education upon which institutions are modeled today (Kitzhaber, *Rhetoric in American Colleges* 16). Cyrus Northrup, president of the University of Minnesota, said in 1901 that Yale professors, themselves products of that same college, "have cherished the Yale ideas and have followed the Yale methods. . . . They have held fast to what was good and been slow to enter new and untried paths. The education that in the past had succeeded in giving men power has seemed good enough for the future" (qtd. in Kitzhaber, *Rhetoric in American Colleges* 26). But economic and social conditions of the early twentieth century created a need for serious reflection upon the circular and insular logic of Yale's long-standing educational philosophy. In eliminating its Latin requirement and altering the entrance examination to better match the current high-school curriculum, Yale did so to

> make it easier for Western high-school students to enter. If that meant sacrificing Latin, or examining in new subjects, or even accepting students on certificate, let the changes be made. . . . [T]he College had hoped to preserve its standards and its influence on the Eastern preparatory schools, while at the same time it opened the way by an alternate door to the high-school men from the West. (Pierson, *Yale College* 510)

Under this proposal, known as "Plan B," the result was "easier examinations and a wider choice" (Pierson, *Yale College* 511). Pierson notes that Yale President George Hadley endorsed this new admissions approach by arguing that plan B would "render greater service by insisting on good methods of study in things that the nation wants to know [rather] than by teaching things it does not want" (qtd. in Pierson, *Yale College* 512), echoing the shift from accumulated knowledge of classical subjects to the implementation of practical training in higher education. Wozniak states, "The college arts curriculum began to take on as much of the university methods of specialization and freedom of choice as the varying financial resources and the varying educational philosophies of the administrators and faculties of the different colleges would allow" (119).

Such amendments to standards at Yale continued into the mid-twentieth century. These amendments were necessary due to, first, the influx of postwar students and, second, the *decrease* in enrollments following the advent of regional and increasingly prestigious western colleges for men who had neither the means nor inclination to travel east. Historian Karabel points out that in 1933, Yale admissions officials "scrap[ed] the bottom of the admissions barrel," admitting "more than one hundred candidates who would have ordinarily been rejected" from the pool, of which 70 percent to 80 percent were usually prep-school graduates. Such desperation stemmed from the continuing Depression and the number of more privileged and better-prepared students declining admission offers, presumably due to a reversal of fortunes (200).

Additionally, during this period between the wars, "a college education became an essential part of the success strategy of those who sought fortune or passage in the United States" as opposed to a pursuit for intellectual edification or a confirmation of one's existing social birthright (Levine 43). Yale's and Harvard's efforts to reach a wider population were, thus, a response to growing societal pressures for *all* young men to attend college—with regional and local colleges, both public and private, being created in response, often with much more accessible programs than those found in the Ivy League.[1]

By the end of the 1930s, the affects of the first wave of changes was clear at Yale:

> Without written, essay-type tests, an institution like Yale could no longer be quite sure of the training or distinguished performance in the preparatory subjects. . . . As for the English tests, without any essay questions to stiffen them, they seemed to let in increasing numbers who could neither read nor spell with any accuracy, and whose semi-illiteracy sometimes drove their college teachers wild . . . As one English instructor remarked, he had never taught students worse trained or with better potential ability. Others thought the best students more mature and competent than ever before, but the weaker students much worse. (Pierson, *Yale* 501–2)

In a January 28, 1935, memo, S. B. Hemingway, then-English-department chair at Yale, suggested to then-provost Charles B. Seymour,

> Sophomore teachers[2] are this year constantly sneering at the laxity of the standards of the Freshman year. Harvard, I believe,

> declines to accept Freshmen who have flunked the C.E.E.B. (College Entrance Examination Board) exam in English. We accept many such, and most of them avoid Freshman English. I would suggest a required Freshman English course, chiefly composition, for all who flunk the entrance examination.

Even though such a course proposal—for a more rhetorical approach to first-year English curricula—carried the right intentions, no course of this type was implemented at Yale.

The idea that over time and with succeeding generations of writers, the bottom gets worse and the top gets better, while the middle goes largely unchanged (and unnoticed) as "average," is still a point of admissions lore at many institutions. Pierson's idea of "worse prepared" but "better potential" students is a pairing that also quite accurately describes many of today's basic writers. By accident of circumstances (here, poor secondary preparation), the writer comes to university not unwilling but temporarily *unable* to do the work of the "average" student. Such lore is also reflected in Mike Rose's discussion of the "myth of transience" in remedial writing instruction, which "assures its believers that the past was better or that the future will be. The turmoil that they are currently in will pass. The source of the problem is elsewhere, thus it can be ignored or temporarily dealt with" ("Language of Exclusion" 355). Perhaps backed by believers in this myth, Yale chose to create a course that existed as a site of necessary (and private) linguistic refinement rather than an integral part of the curriculum. This course existed as such an always-temporary presence, serving a purely corrective and acculturating function as an appendage to, rather than a component of, Yale's larger English program.

THE "AWKWARD" NATURE OF REMEDIAL WRITERS: YALE'S PLAN

Awkward squad:

> "A squad of inexperienced recruits led by a non-commissioned officer for the purpose of instruction" (http://abuffalosoldier.com/slang.htm).

> "British slang for people who are inexperienced, clumsy or insubordinate" (http://www.probertencyclopaedia.com/cgi-bin/xphrase.pl?keyword=awkward+squad).

As early as 1912, the term *awkward squad* was being applied by the larger English studies community to underprepared writers. Students in need of "remedial" instruction, or those students relegated to the lowest rung of writing coursework, were designated as "awkward squad" members within first-year writing curricula. Although the term was equated with "the gymnasium class" for physically unfit juvenile delinquents in detention facilities and other settings (Nibecker 80; Ross 150), it soon became associated with academic remedial instruction. In his 1912 article "Elasticity in Freshman English Courses," Philip H. Churchman employs what may be the earliest published use of the term in composition studies when he proposes that in "Subdividing a typical Freshman class of, say, 100 men into various grades . . . we might discover three or more categories: for instance, the elite (the upper 25), the average (the middle 50) and the awkward squad" (309). Russell notes that in 1915, Harvard had a "foreign squad, an awkward squad, and sections for the rest who showed no great infirmities" (150). Outside English, in other subjects, this term was also used to refer to inexperienced or underprepared students; in an article advocating for postgraduate study in the classics—so as to avoid the "grind" of teaching high school—one instructor commented, "After the most painstaking instruction and the simplest hay-foot, straw-foot methods, we find a goodly number of our awkward squad eternally out of step" (Delcamp 449).

The origins of the term stem from the parlance of the British Army, wherein the "awkward squad" stood for unprepared, ill-trained soldiers, led by an equally unfit commanding officer. The term was also used in the American Armed Forces, to designate troops in need of further training before entering battle, as "any army man can testify that no healthy recruit was ever injured by the 'setting up' drills or 'awkward squad' work necessary to establish that clean, soldierly carriage so noticeable even in the military cots" ("Educational News" 267).

This label as applied to remedial writers thus obviously had similar negative connotations, as a term of ridicule and signal for needed refinement. The desire for a metaphorical "clean, soldierly carriage" in first-year writers would have been especially intense at an institution of privilege and social breeding such as Yale. Such a label would have also had a familiar, regimented ring to it, especially to academics teaching during the first two World Wars and in all-male environments, where military terminology was well-known and had already been absorbed into the vernacular.[3]

For many years prior to World War II, the standard first-year English course at Yale—which asked students to read and discuss select pieces from the literary canon, without focusing significantly on writing instruction—was not required of entering students but was still elected by about 95 percent of the class (Johnson, "Politics of Back to Basics" 3). Thus, the remedial course, or Awkward Squad, was not a placement mechanism or even a prerequisite to the first-year literary course but rather an amorphous site to which students were *remanded* by their writing instructor. The course had no official institutional recognition; its students had no support beyond the tutors who drilled them weekly in spelling and grammar until such time as they were deemed fit to be allowed back into the mainstream (Johnson, "Politics of Back to Basics" 3). The basic course changed names throughout the next forty years. From my study of the *Yale Undergraduate Courses of Study* and other related materials from 1919 to 1951, the basic writing course existed as a post-hoc placement designation throughout—that is, as a site of instruction to which students could be remanded for "poor performance"—but was only cited as a Yale course in three academic years during this period, under the titles English 1A, 10, and 10–5. By contrast, the *standard* first-year course occupied a great many course numbers and permutations—with a different course number nearly every year.

But the designation for underprepared writers remained, if only known to those maintaining the English studies curriculum. As Paula Johnson, also working from the Yale archives, comments, "I came to the conclusion that the favorite pastime of university professors is rearranging the curriculum. Though the syllabus of

Yale's freshman English only underwent one change of any significance in two-thirds of a century, other courses sprang up and died away around it, and other aspects of the basic course itself, equally important to it as a basis, did change" ("Politics of Back to Basics" 3). Based on my review of these same materials, I concur: nearly every year between 1929 and 1945, the basic curriculum changed just enough to merit an entirely renumbered listing of the lower-division courses alone.

One contemporary article outlining Yale's Awkward Squad passionately defends its curriculum and academic success; another article makes lesser claims about the course, citing a distanced perspective from its curriculum but provides hope of its eventual dissolution. Each piece is worth parsing to see how this remedial course and its students were regarded in the local setting.

The first, eponymous article, written by Carroll S. Towle[4] in 1929 for *English Journal*, characterizes the students populating the course in this manner: "Amused tolerance, outward sullenness, inward rebellion, ignorant earnestness, pathetic anxiety—it takes all these to make an Awkward Squad" (672). Towle's article describes the curriculum for the squad and the procedures by which students are admitted into—and released from—its confines. Towle, however, cannot provide any kind of exact rubric for what constitutes the experience in or the end results of enrollment in the Awkward Squad:

> Does this selection mean failure in the regular English work? How much time will such extra-curriculum work require? Will it all seem too dull and arduous, a burden which is first cousin to the "last straw"? Several years of studying English composition having proved to be of small value, will this new attempt be worthwhile? There can be no doubt that such questions are in the minds of the group generally as they sit expectant. (672)

Towle admits that students come to the course with a variety of feelings about their placement as well: "Some of the most inarticulate are willing to learn and to practice what should be done; their fellows may be positive that their own presence in the Squad constitutes rank injustice" (672). Again, parallels are evident in the diversity of experience in basic writing courses nationwide; as tempting as it might be to label all basic writing students as one "type," it cannot be done—not even in an otherwise fairly uniform population (here all white men of relative financial privilege) such as the Awkward Squad. For this reason, Towle emphasizes the individually focused pedagogy, stating, "We certainly should not wish any students to feel that their time is being sacrificed to aid another solely; each [student] must be made to feel that his own difficulties are being in some measure duly considered and analyzed" (673).

Certain aspects of the course, however, were clearly uniform. The Awkward Squad was designed as a drill course, emphasizing spelling, punctuation, and "grosser mistakes in sentence structure" (673). Towle is clear that the squad "must never become a studied review of formal English composition"; thus, the squad was seemingly designed as a rote drilling of mechanics rather than a site for broader writing practice. The Awkward Squad met weekly with a spelling test "at practically each meeting" (673). There was no work outside of class but "almost invariably the students write a theme in class each week . . . primarily for the correction of actual errors" rather than to advance expository writing skills (674). Towle notes that this workload keeps the student from complaining that "too much of his time is required." No grades were given; however, students did spend ten minutes each week in a conference to discuss "three or four errors . . . picking those which need attention first" (674).

Second is E. S. Noyes's brief article "The Program of the Awkward Squad," published the following month in *English Journal*. Noyes begins his piece: "There is practically no composition in the regular Freshman English course at Yale," thus setting the stage for a discussion of the Awkward Squad as a highly contrasting setting to the standard first-year course, wherein writing practice is not a regular activity. Noyes echoes Towle's discussion of the variability of squad enrollees by admitting, "No doubt the standard by which assignments are made varies somewhat among the instructors; each is left free to send as many Freshman to the Squad as he thinks need the drill." Noyes emphasizes that students of all entrance exam scores are admitted to the squad, without instructor prior knowledge of these scores (678). In making these two admissions, Noyes exposes the subjectivity of squad student "placement" as well as the poor correlation between test scores and actual writing ability—especially in the absence of an objective standard for the course (or placement into it).

Noyes elaborates on the actual structure of the course: there were actually two squads—one for spelling drills only, encompassing men who have "no other outstanding faults of technique," and one for the "generally deficient," who need more overall assistance in writing (678). This observation exposes a two-tier structure within the squad course, though it is not clear that those with spelling problems are any quicker studies or are considered more easily "fixed" than their counterparts. Ultimately, Noyes states that "once in the Squad, a man stays until he is cured," invoking the medical terminology so widely used to describe remedial writers in this era. If a writer, further, "suffers a relapse" later in the year, he may be remanded back to the squad as well (679).

The most notable element of Noyes's piece is his closing hope that the Awkward Squad will be a temporary reality only at Yale. He posits that the squad "like the Indian, seems to be vanishing" as the enrollment had fallen from 175 to 125 in the space of one academic year (679), due to factors, Noyes believes, of better secondary preparation, comprehensive entrance testing, and "some general rise in the standard of Freshman" (680). Such hypotheses would seem to indicate that Noyes was woefully out of touch with the climate for admissions and high-school-to-college connections during this time—as the influences he cites were viewed by others as reasons *for* a rise in remedial writing courses. Ultimately, the squad not only did *not* disappear but *gained* members at Yale as the years went by, enrolling nearly a quarter of the freshman class by midcentury.

Although the structure and purpose of the Awkward Squad time are obviously not progressive ones—with the emphasis on mechanics and error rather than intellectual engagement with writing itself—the individual attention paid to the students is an interesting predecessor to the pedagogy found in many basic writing programs today. Emphasizing the need to speak with *each* student individually shows a level of attention admirable in its intent and in contrast to other instruction in the Ivy League during this time. For example, as JoAnn Campbell argues, at Radcliffe in the 1910s and 1920s, English A was neither beneficial nor challenging. Campbell notes that English A students had one idea of the purpose of the first-year writing class and its teachers had another. English A for these women not only violated what they thought the purpose of a college education was—to develop the ability to learn what was thought and to express one's ideas—but the pedagogical practices violated these women's understanding of how human beings should be treated (474). Campbell further comments, "The banking theory of education was alive and well at the turn of the century (a professor's knowledge and power was absolute and any cultural capital the student brought into the classroom was checked at the door)" (475).

I cannot argue, of course, that the format of the Awkward Squad allowed for students to gain this important "cultural capital" lost in the recitation model of early Ivy League instruction. Nor would I attempt to claim that gender discrimination had nothing to do with the Radcliffe women's negative experiences in the classroom. But it is interesting to note that the individual approach to instruction—treating these men, indeed, *as* individuals—is at the core of the squad's design, perhaps due to the politically conservative desire to personally cultivate young men for positions of community leadership (which surely entailed proficiency in speech and writing). It should be noted that this individual approach remained in the first-year writing curriculum throughout the twentieth century, with student-professor conferences a central feature of the first-year course in each of its permutations.

A structure such as this was not necessarily common, however, across other remedial courses at other institutions; for example, in his 1939 *College English* piece, W. Alan Grove notes that his time- and labor-saving approach to writing conferences is to gather groups of students together who are having similar writing problems and speak with them as a collective, as "the value of conferences cannot be overestimated, but to attempt personal ones would be absurd" (232). As evidence of the conferencing tradition within Yale's larger composition program, an October 1936 memo from then-chair of English, S. B. Hemingway to the provost requests "another $600 for Freshmen [English 10] theme conferences [which] would properly relieve four overburdened Freshman instructors." This instruction was obviously taxing; Hemingway says, without any irony, these instructors "are used to being imposed upon, so I put their claims last."[5]

This individual instruction did not guarantee immediate success for all writers enrolled in the squad, however. The squad instructors were

> content when the instructor agrees that the student's writing appears in general to be free of downright errors and reasonably comprehensible. Then the man is released. A few are held for individual attention the next year; these have their grade in the regular English withheld until such time as their writing approximates the general standard. (Towle 677)

The design of the squad, then—to serve as an early version of a "lab" attached to the first-year course—evidences its position in the curriculum and may explain its noninclusion in the course catalogues of the time. Students' performances in the squad bore *direct weight* upon the grade received in the general writing course; students who failed the squad were required to be held back for the following year. Thus, the course was not a freestanding *prerequisite* for students unable to do the work of the first-semester course; instead, it was a freeform appendage to the course itself, designed to allow fluid enrollments and no official remedial "placement."

In its design, the Awkward Squad prefigured the structure of other remedial programs in the United States later in the century, such as the program at the University of Illinois at Chicago (UIC) in the early 1960s, whereby students who made repeated errors in grammar, spelling, or usage could be given a "yellow slip," which would refer them to the English department for assistance with remedial work (Masters 36). A similar "calling out" approach was used at Wheaton College in the 1950s, with a threefold checklist for students, urging them, in each of the three options, to "write with more care" (Masters 39). As Masters notes, these admonitions on the part of Wheaton College suggest that remedial students "knew the law [of grammar], but disregarded it, like motorists who run stop signs or ignore the speed limit" (40). At Yale, in contrast, there is no direct evidence that Awkward Squad students were regarded as "careless" so much as simply *unfortunates*—those who needed to be kept out of regular instruction until they could be remade as "regular" literate Yale men. Nonetheless, these general methodologies of separation and classification take their cues from the squad's overall remediation plan—though it is unlikely that officials at UIC or Wheaton knew of Yale's plan, given its relatively buried history and indeterminate scope at Yale.

In fact, the number of students and "repeaters" in the squad throughout this period and the variant forms (spelling drills only, for example) that these students took was often too difficult to measure, even inside the Awkward Squad population itself. In the "Annual Report of the English Department, Yale University, 1929–1930," George Nettleton states, "Freshmen English (including repeaters, 'Awkward Squad,' etc.)" constituted on average 950–1000 enrollees per academic year, but "chiefly on account of the variations of the 'Awkward Squad,' these figures are only approximate." Thirty years later, in 1959, Chairman Louis L. Martz reported that enrollment in the Awkward Squad, now "English 10, designed to perform remedial work in composition" was "about 130 per year" compared to "about 430" students enrolled in English 15, the standard first-year course ("Annual Report of the Department of English to the President, 1958–1959").

Secondary materials of the time also reference Yale's approach to and curricular revisions for basic writing students. Among these materials are William C. Devane's extensive detailing of "The New Program in Yale College" in April 1947, and J. O. Bailey's piece on Yale's, Harvard's, and Princeton's first-year writing curricula in February 1946. Bailey "cites the *Yale Report of the Committee on the Course of Study* and its description of 'English 10'"—the later version of the squad. English 10 "planned to teach the freshmen to read and write English with facility and clarity"; about "20% of the students [are] exempted . . . based on high grades through four years of high school English and an honors grade on the tests for college entrance" (7). Bailey notes that at these three universities, "the course in freshman composition is considered something below college level, a nuisance, but a necessity for most students" (7). Still, he concludes, "[The Ivy League schools] are thinking fundamentally about these problems, and some of their suggestions are well worth our pondering" (8). Bailey's comment echoes other pressing comparisons of the time, for example the query, "If Yale students are deficient in the art of composition, what are the students of institutions with less rigorous standards of admission?" (Sparling 68). It is important to note that in the earlier half of the twentieth century, composition studies was a new enterprise, the study of basic writing not yet a subdiscipline. Faculty raised on Great Books and other pedagogical models of the late nineteenth century were faced with a new type of student—in need of a new type of curriculum—and were daunted by this prospect.

One new type of student was the returning soldier, an enrollment phenomenon also mentioned by Robin Varnum in her study of Amherst College. During World War II, Yale took great pains to accommodate this type of student, even producing special wartime versions of its course bulletin, which included provisions for servicemen either starting or finishing their degrees under the Army Specialized Training Program, connected explicitly to the GI Bill. One such accommodation was the allowance for typical fall-semester-only courses to be offered in spring semester as well to provide accessible enrollment for midyear registrants back from duty. Another significant accommodation was the creation of "Basic English for the Army Specialized Training Program," a specially designed version of the basic writing course for these returning soldiers.[6] The basic course of World War II years, at this point labeled English 10-5, was on Yale's bulletins in 1941; it is mentioned in this year as part of a budget request to "take care of Hess's division of English 10-5; the consultant work for the English majors in Berkeley College; and the paper reading in English 22." The course must have served a significant number of students, because in a memo dated January 22, 1942, Stanley T. Williams asks Provost Edward Furniss for support in requesting a "Deferment in the Military Service" for Dudley R. Johnson, who "teaches English

10-5, a course in which spelling, writing, and other forms of English composition receive particular attention." Williams asserts that it will be "very difficult" to find a substitute for this course should Johnson leave, indicating both the need for the course to run (as opposed to being cancelled for lack of staff) *and* the specialized nature of instruction within the course, instruction that many were apparently not qualified to undertake.

A syllabus for the basic skills/army course was devised by the Yale Freshman Committee and presented to Provost Furniss in May 1943. The one-page document outlines four goals: "(1) to write accurately and effectively; (2) to read with preciseness and understanding; (3) to speak in public with confidence and effectiveness; (4) to listen with attention and understanding" (Yale Freshman Committee 1943). Writing progressed from grammar review in term 1, to "a study of their words and functions" in term 2, to "a study of the principles of exposition, argumentation, and persuasion" in term 3. Reading went from "selections to illustrate various sorts of description," to "close study of selections of imaginative literature," to "close study of selections illustrating the principles of exposition, argumentation, and persuasion." Speaking areas focused on speeches and oral exercises, with little variance across the three terms. Listening was taught through exercises in dictation. The structure of this course plan, including the introduction of literature near the end of the course, matches closely with George S. Wykoff's description of a similar course at Purdue University in 1945, which served not only returning soldiers but also new high-school graduates and others who "had passed [Purdue's] own Army English course" but who were compelled to repeat the Basic course due to failure of other non-English subjects, assumedly on the basis of struggling writing ability ("Army English Experiences" 338).

This course plan is ambitious and comprehensive; it aims not only to teach students the basics of grammar and mechanics but also eventually argumentation and persuasion, all the while *also* teaching literary appreciation, public-speaking skills, and note-taking. If an instructor today attempted all of these activities in one term, he or she might be laughed out of the department. But the intensity of this syllabus shows the emergence of the modern expository writing course in its attention to modes and argumentation; it also shows the evolution of a curriculum that had once prioritized literature and *not* composition but now sees the value of combining these two pursuits, albeit in one very packed course. English 10-5 was designed to meet the very *practical* needs of these men who were reentering American society. But still it was labeled "Basic Skills," likely because it diverged from the traditional literary curriculum.[7]

In these ways, the Ivy League would seem to be setting a precedent for handling lower-level, underprepared writing students and other specialized populations well before the programs documents in the better-known studies of basic writing curricula at public or open-admissions universities. The prevailing argument for studying this particular curricula, then, seems to be that if students are struggling at the Ivy League, then they are struggling everywhere. As far as the opposite of this model goes—the Ivies seeking models *elsewhere* for how to assist first-year writers—Paula Johnson has commented, "Faculties 'in here' [Yale] agree that students should write well; but they often recoil from suggestions that we might learn—might even learn from the invisible desert called 'elsewhere'—to teach writing more effectively" ("Freshman English in the Ivy League" 14). Nevertheless, Yale served as a model *location* for offering instruction in remedial writing, a model made much more public at Harvard and more explicitly emulated by other institutions, a phenomenon discussed in chapter 5.

Without looking at primary materials, however, it is extremely difficult to grasp the complete linear history of basic writing at Yale. Even within the archives, there is little explicit discussion of the Awkward Squad or its inheritors; instead, such discussions come under larger curricular initiatives, brief narratives by department chairs or other faculty, or intercollege memos. I have attempted to reconstruct these bits and pieces of evidence, with the caveat that out of the historical context, some of the import is surely lost. I concur with Lisa Ede in this respect, who argues, "Conventional hierarchies of knowledge position scholars as experts and teachers as practitioners. . . . [S]cholars have the authority to abstract and generalize, to distinguish what *seems* to be the case and what is *really* true. This authority is often denied to teachers, who are authorized primarily to speak about their own students and classrooms" (139). I regret that my research—partly due to the number of years that have passed since these classes were taught and partly due to the lack of available course records detailing the aggregate names of students and faculty alike in the Awkward Squad sections—does not allow any past teachers of basic writing at Yale to speak for themselves. I also regret that a full archival collection for the Department of English does not exist at Yale, as such documentation would allow certain gaps to be filled in.

Nonetheless, the collected evidence and aggregate voices—culled from a variety of administrative levels—suggest a deeply conflicted and ever-creative English department and college administration where first-year studies was concerned, with correspondence and curricular revisions evidencing an ongoing struggle to answer the question, "Where do these writers *belong* at an institution like ours?" This is a question not limited, I contend, to Yale alone, because although the characteristics of "underprepared" Ivy League writers obviously differ from the definition given to such students at less-elite institutions, their social stratification within the institutional structure is rhetorically similar. As David Bartholomae notes, the classification of "basic writing" has historically "mark[ed] an uneasy accommodation between the institution and its desires and a student body that did not or would not fit" ("Remedial Writing Courses" 8). Similarly, Rose comments, "[T]he notion of remediation . . . serves to exclude from the academic community those who are so labeled. They sit in scholastic quarantine until their disease can be diagnosed and remedied" ("Language of Exclusion" 352). Basic writers in the Ivy League, however, may be regarded with even *more* disdain and sometimes more isolation than their public university (two- and four-year) counterparts, due to local, institutional values.

For example, Joseph W. Gordon and Linda H. Peterson point out that even the notion of creating a central writing *laboratory* had remedial connotations, and "[r]emedial . . . is an obscene word at Yale" (14). Anywhere from 6 to 10 percent of writers in the Ivy

League, including at Yale, historically were internally and institutionally classified as "remedial" through the late 1970s (Johnson and Hackman 228; Johnson, "Freshman English" 15). Johnson notes that the terms *remedial* and *basic* often "are not [synonymous]; [but] at an Ivy League school, they are" ("Freshman English" 16). In other words, whereas some institutions classify their first-semester course as the "introductory" course in composition, at Yale and elsewhere in the Ivy League, such study has historically been categorized as below admission standards, with the systematic study of literature and literary models the focus of the introductory course. Within any larger "basic" category are also those students in need of additional help with the true basics of writing—including mechanics. But in the Ivy League, as Johnson asserts, there has generally not been a systematic tutoring or support system for general writing practice, as is in place at other schools, for example, Stanford University, where departmental officials can thus "afford to 'place down' many more students than can colleges where only tutors are available to help those who write poorly" ("Freshman English" 15).

This distinction is critical when considering the archival materials that delineate basic writing and basic writers during these early years of the twentieth century. While certainly some of the students in remedial courses had significant structural issues in their writing, most likely many were simply underprepared in the skills of written literary analysis. This is not to argue that such literature-based courses are without value or that all colleges who have such a curriculum would demarcate a good number of their students as "basic." But in the particular local context of Yale during this time, the argument that the mastery of expository writing should be a pre-college activity is germane to any argument about who constituted the basic writers at Yale and why.

Take, for example, the piece "English at Yale," written in 1924 by department chair Nettleton for the *Yale Alumni Weekly.* Nettleton reinforces the subservient relationship of composition to literature at Yale during this time as he describes the first-semester course:

> (1) it is a course in *literature,* not in *composition;* (2) it selects a few representative authors for careful reading, without at-

> tempting a general survey of English literature as a whole; (3) it emphasizes appreciation of literature, not the acquisition of facts or linguistic discipline. It differs radically from what many regard as the normal Freshman English course—elementary composition work. ("English at Yale" 1062)

Nettleton goes on to clarify where the Awkward Squad fits into this first-year paradigm:

> It should be added that since the merger of the separate Freshman courses of Yale college and the Scientific School, Freshman English has had an "Awkward Squad," in which are placed for special drill those who are deficient in training or ability to write. Practice in writing and personal theme-conferences form part also of the regular work. . . . Freshman English is still maintained in harmony with the cultural tradition of the past. Its main aim is to stimulate intelligent appreciation of literature. ("English at Yale" 1062)

Nettleton is quick to point out that the study of literature is prioritized over the study of writing and that this focus sets Yale apart from other institutions. He also takes pains to clarify the origins of the remedial course, implicitly putting blame on the students from Yale's Scientific (Engineering) School—although no archival evidence supports this contention. This trend toward labeling the remedial course for "special" students, however, *does* continue in archival materials throughout the early 1950s. The most telling part of Nettleton's piece is the last two sentences, about maintaining "harmony" with the past and stressing "intelligent appreciation of literature." Nettleton strives to characterize the first-year course as *anything but* composition, clearly positioned as drudgery against the "intelligent" work of literary study. This uneasy relationship between composition and literature is, of course, nothing new, but in the case of Yale's writing courses, such a relationship intensifies the stratification of (and widens the criteria for) remedial instruction. It also further, arguably unfairly, labels the pursuit of "regular" writing as something that should be clearly separate from the higher-order pursuit of literature. In promoting this relationship in its English offerings, Yale parroted the split that reportedly began with the inception of Harvard's English A, which Susan Miller asserts caused the "two pursuits of literature and composition [to be] joined immediately as 'high' and 'low'" (53).

The following chapter describes the comparable remedial writing program at Harvard University during this time, a program that stands in clear contrast to Yale's Awkward Squad, both in design and in public status. Through a complex but precise and thoughtful construction of post–English A coursework, Harvard University, in staying true to its infamous heritage as the "birthplace" of first-year English composition, appears to also have been one of the originators of the modern *basic* writing program as well.

5

Beyond English A: Harvard's Basic Writers and "Fatherly" Advice

> Good English is required both in spoken and written work, not only in English courses but in all courses. Any student whose work is unsatisfactory in English, whether in the details of spelling or grammar or in the larger matter of clear expression of ideas, is reported to the Committee on the Use of English by Students, and may be required to receive special instruction intended to correct these deficiencies. Such special work will in no case be counted as a course for the degree.
>
> —Harvard University *Courses of Instruction*, Fall 1950

SCHOLARS IN COMPOSITION STUDIES have extensively studied first-year writing at Harvard University, or "English A," many going so far as to attribute the beginning of modern composition to this institutional location.[1] Its history has, thus, been well documented, but it is helpful in the context of a study of remedial writing at Harvard to briefly review the rationale for the inception of English A before deeply examining how and where remediation was located within the English department as well as within the institution at large.

Because the archives at Harvard include a vast array of documents cataloging the English department and its individual programs and because the documentation for remedial writing instruction is separately archived, in most instances, within the trappings of a particular series of committees, the archivist seeking clarification on remedial writing at Harvard has a relatively streamlined path to follow. Ultimately, the portrait of remedial writing at Harvard emerges as an ironically proud enterprise led by several persevering individuals who sought to groom young men as gracious, gentlemanly scholars who would represent Harvard to the academic and general public.

ENGLISH A: THE FIRST "GREAT WAVE"?

In an essay written in 1879, Adams Sherman Hill outlines the one-hour English Entrance Examination, which tested students' writing ability on one of the following five subjects: "(I) The character of Sir Richard Steele; (II) The Duke of Marlborough as portrayed by Thackeray; (III) The style of 'Henry Esmond'; (IV) Thackeray's account of the Pretender's visit to England; and (V) Dueling in the Age of Queen Anne" (9).Clearly, entering Harvard students needed not only to exhibit fluency in language and thought but also mastery of literary knowledge and elite cultural histories, similar to the skills required of Yale entering students during this era. As Hill describes, Harvard faculty found 157 students' work on the examination to be of a failing nature in 1879, for reasons ranging from "ignorance of subject matter" to "ignorance of punctuation" (9–10). Hill asserts that in order to fail the exam, a writer "had to commit several serious faults" (10), concluding that "overall, the examination makes a poor showing for the schools that furnish the material whereof the university which professes to set up the highest standard in America" (11).[2] Thereafter, the English A course was born at Harvard both as a response to and defense against any perception that Harvard would harbor—or ultimately allow itself to produce—anything less than gentlemen possessing "an excellent and refined use of the mother tongue" (Hill, "Answers" 7).

In his groundbreaking *Composition-Rhetoric: Backgrounds, Theory, and Pedagogy*, Robert Connors notes that English A began in 1885 and by 1886 was taught by eight instructors (185). English A replaced the required sophomore writing course initiated by Hill and in doing so, Connors argues, was an instigator of the "first great wave of college level remedial English" (129). English A addressed "the illiteracy of American boys" through the 1870s across the United States (Connors 129). The course "was considered remedial and was bitterly resented by college faculty members," who assumed "that freshman composition courses were a stopgap remedial measure, a temporary aberration, to be dispensed with after the great propaganda war in favor of more secondary school composition had been won" (185). But such hopes were short-sighted. By 1890, "freshman composition was the rule at most schools," not just Harvard (Connors 187), thereby solidifying Harvard's historical reputation as the "birthplace" of first-year composition and beginning the early modern history of this course of study at the collegiate level.[3]

Connors uses Harvard as a prime example of the kind of instruction emerging during the "Postwar and Consolidation periods" between 1865 and 1900, wherein the fact that "college composition was fast becoming error-obsessed was like a shameful secret . . . mentioned only obliquely" (130). He contends that most teachers of rhetoric were loathe to admit to or openly deal with problems of grammar, instead asking for "deliverance by some sort of secondary school *deus ex pedagogia*" (131). At least two lasting components of modern composition curricula were born of this denial: First, the grammar handbook began to emerge in the early 1900s, as a shorthand method of addressing students' surface difficulties (Connors 146), and, second, instructors began to occasionally assign more personal, facile topics for writing, scrapping the "abstract topics" popular in previous eras (Connors 41). Such personal work "could be quickly scanned for obvious flaws" (Connors 146) thus reducing the teaching of composition to instruction in correctness at the surface level, which prevails in many less-progressive college writing programs today and is certainly evident writ large within the curricular confines of secondary-school writing instruction.

Despite Connors's widely regarded history of English A, however, far less has been investigated regarding *actual* remedial composition at Harvard, or pre/sub–English A courses. Even within this scholarly discussion of what critics might now call the original "dumbing-down" of writing curricula to serve the exigent circumstances of local teachers and students as well as nationwide cultural predilections and social anxieties regarding literacy and correctness, Connors's landmark study does not discuss the several remedial efforts that were an outgrowth of English A at Harvard—namely English C, D, and F. These were courses that served students who performed poorly in English A, who showed poorly on the entrance examination as transfer students into Harvard, or who were simply determined by their instructors to have additional need for practice in expository writing, even if they had passed English A with high marks.

These courses are rarely discussed in contemporary composition studies scholarship. One exception is David Russell, who notes that in 1914, the Committee on the Use of English by Students at Harvard was formed, as it was found that "writing skills declined after English A" (150). As such, the committee was further charged with the task of "mending English at Harvard" (qtd. in 150). Russell argues that the course born of this "typical and quite influential" committee's work—English F (also at various times designated English C and D, as evident from Harvard archival records)—is powerful evidence that

> language instruction was not a question of fostering social or intellectual development but of treating a social or mental illness (as the medical terminology suggests). Remediation found a permanent place within the new comprehensive schools and colleges because, unlike many other cooperation schemes, it reinforced the institutional structure. Institutions gained a means of sorting students into groups that could be taught (or not taught) a certain set of linguistic conventions tied to future occupations and life-styles. The writing police and remedial courses allowed all faculty to share responsibility for language standards without sharing responsibility for language instruction, which remained with English instructors (usually with low status) and preserved the differentiated curriculum. (151–52)

While I agree with Russell's general argument that remedial instruction served to reinforce the status quo of English programs and larger institutions, especially when viewed through the "social sorting" function that Tom Fox criticizes, I also maintain that at Harvard, there were, in fact, significant "social development" aims in the creation and maintenance of English C, D, and F—aims that are evident from archival documents that discuss and debate these courses' existence. Particularly when set beside the somewhat secretive and certainly punitively constructed Awkward Squad for remedial writers at Yale, Harvard's approach to remedial writing in the first half of the twentieth century evidences a much more progressive approach to lower-level writing instruction. While English C, D, and F were sites to which students were frequently remanded for additional instruction in expository writing, part of what one might call the wait-and-see approach to the offer of remedial or basic writing instruction that was also at work in Yale's Awkward Squad, Harvard's remedial offerings were neither secret in standing nor overtly punitive in design. Further, even though English A at Harvard did include some analysis of literary texts, its main purpose was the practice of exposition and clear prose/argument—as opposed to Yale's course, which was (and remains to this day) purely a course in writing *about* literature.

This chapter discusses Harvard's remedial writing courses as offered between 1920 and 1960, using archival evidence from course catalogues and course plans/curricula, student perceptions of the course published in the *Harvard Crimson* and elsewhere, and documents and records of the Committee on the Use of English by Students, mentioned by Russell. In addition, I look at the position of the English C, D and F courses in the larger context of the growth and refinement, and eventual dismantling (in favor of first the General Education program and later the Harvard Expository Writing program) of the original English A course. The remedial coursework provided and, in some cases, mandated by Harvard was as much an effort to produce the ideal "Harvard Gentleman" as it was an effort to reinforce the importance of "accurate recording of thought" (Russell 151) in expository writing. Harvard's English C, D, and F courses were part of a more enlightened writing course sequence that while ultimately constructed to breed gentleman writers fit to wear the Harvard name also demonstrated a more diversified attitude toward ability grouping and layered curricular goals than its Ivy League counterpart and chief competitor, Yale University.

WHAT'S IN A NAME? TRACKING "SPECIAL INSTRUCTION" AT HARVARD

Between 1914 and 1950, Harvard offered three different types of nonstandard writing courses for its composition students. These courses were an English as a Second Language composition course, a remedial writing course, and a "special instruction" course, which was not a formal course at all but a curricular, on-the-books provision for individually arranged conferences and instruction, not unlike the Awkward Squad's structure at Yale.[4] The remedial course proper was typically the site to which students were remanded based on poor performance in English A or other intake measurements, such as the entrance examination. The "special instruction" course was a variation on the remedial course, designed as an elective site for students wishing "more preparation" in writing as well as students whose difficulties with writing were reported by their instructors across the curriculum. The special instruction course also occasionally included graduate students or upper-level students who sought help improving their writing prior to senior exams or final projects.

Harvard's composition course structure and labeling of courses is far more complicated than that found at Yale during this time but also is far more transparent for historians and archivists, particularly the documentation of the "special instruction" curricula. Even though Yale changed the name of its first-year writing course multiple times during this period, its remedial course was rarely listed in public documents,. At Harvard, in contrast, each of the offered composition courses is listed in the course catalogs and described in full in the yearly bulletins throughout the years in which they were on the books.

Because the course labels (A, A-1, A-2, Aa, Ab, B, C, D, F) change frequently over this time period, sometimes for only short spans of time, it may assist readers to refer to table 1. Note that both the remedial course and the "special instruction" course were eliminated from course catalogs after 1948, immediately prior to the introduction of the general education curriculum. Comparatively, during the 1950s at Yale, while there are still institutional, internal references to Awkward Squad students, a similar curricular shift occurs with the heightened popularity of "Daily Themes" courses, which supplant traditional composition and begin to include options such as creative writing in their focus (and creative writers as the instructors of record, for example, Robert Penn Warren). The remedial course at Harvard reemerged briefly once during the subsequent decade, in 1966–67. After the birth of the Harvard Expository Writing program in 1970–71, a lower-level composition course appears, Expos 10, which continues as the prestandard composition course at Harvard into the twenty-first-century curriculum, though it is not considered remedial in its design or objectives.[5] Despite the absence of formal course offerings in remedial composition or "special instruction" post-1950, however, the 1950 *Courses of Instruction* clearly evidences the presence of assistance for students with additional needs in writing instruction, as quoted in the epigraph of the current chapter; in addition, references to the work of the Committee on the Use of English by Students continues well into the mid-1950s, in publications such as the *Harvard Crimson.*

Remedial Writing (English D as well as A-2 and A-1) had a mission and target population distinct from "special instruction" in writing (English F or C). The course descriptions for each varied slightly across the years, but the following chronological overview,

Table 1.
Composition courses offered at Harvard University, 1917–60

Year of Instruction	Standard composition course	Remedial course	"Special instruction"	ESL course
1917–29	English A	English D	English F	English E
1929–34	English A-1	English A-2	English F	English E
1934–41	English A	English A-1	English C	English B
1941–43	English A	English D	English C	English B
1943–47	English Aa/Ab	English D	English C	English B
1947–48	English Aa/Ab	none	none	English B
1948–50	English A	none	none	none
1950–60	General Education	none	none	none

gathered from the archived Harvard course bulletins, provides a general overview of course goals, prerequisites, and format.

In 1917, English D and English F were listed in that year's *Course Bulletin* as follows:

> English D (English Composition): "Course D is prescribed for those students in Harvard College who have taken or anticipated Course A, but have not been relieved of prescription. It may be taken in either half-year. It cannot be counted as elective work" (28).
>
> English F (Special Instruction in Writing): "Students who have been relieved of regular prescription of composition, but whose writing is found to be unsatisfactory, may be required by the Committee on the Use of English by Students to take Course F. The course cannot be counted for a degree" (28).

The courses remain as described above from 1917 through 1925, at which point the description for Course F changes slightly: "There is no charge for tuition" and "Work may begin at any time during the college year" (*1925 Course Bulletin* 25). In 1927, the description for English D was modified: "a limited number of (a) students who have passed English A without a grade of distinction and who desire further training in order to qualify themselves for English 31 or 22 [advanced writing courses] and (b) to Freshmen who have gained exemption from English A" (*Course Bulletin* 25). The D course mainly served students who, having completed English A, were determined to "need further prescription of English composition" and were assigned to take English D "in the ensuing year in addition to their regular elective coursework" (*Course Bulletin* 24).

Two years later, in 1929, the rhetorical construct of English D changes in an interesting way. First, it is renamed English A-2, to follow the renaming of English A as English A-1. The course is now described as "a *more advanced course* in writing, designed for Freshman who have obtained a grade of at least 75% on their entrance examination in English" but who want more training to qualify for English 31 or 22, as well as any sophomores who passed English A-1 but want further training/instruction (*Course Bulletin* 25, italics mine). The stigma of remediation is absent from this course; indeed, it is no longer constructed by the department as remedial at all but rather *assistive* in its aims. Students who were found to be lacking what instructors found to be effective writing skills were still being remanded to English F, but the separate course that served as a freestanding site for poorly performing students would now be recast as a more desirable offering, strangely mixing (potentially) those students of high ability with those of lower or more average abilities in writing.

Ten years later, however, in 1939, English C was added to the curriculum, apparently replacing (in name) the English F course as the site to which students were remanded for further instruction. English C is similar to English F in previous years' course bulletins but now also is designed for students "who have passed English A with a grade of D" or students whose use of English is determined to be "unsatisfactory in any course" (*Course Bulletin* 29). Just two years following, in 1941, the rhetorical framework of the English C course was reduced to simple symbolic logic: English D was now specifically (and somewhat pejoratively) designed and required for students who received a *grade* of D in English A (*Course Bulletin* 70). It also now carried a "maximum of $50.00" tuition charge, following the growing national climate for added-cost remedial courses at the university level.

Such continued shifts in description, course labels, and course rationales may seem odd—or just unnecessarily complicated—on the surface. But a closer examination of the workings of the Harvard faculty committee behind these remedial offerings, the Committee on the Use of English by Students, reveals both the immense pride taken in offering these varied opportunities for struggling students and an occasional anxiety over obtaining faculty and student support for the courses and the overall program. Though archival evidence clearly indicates that the committee had the best intentions in providing sub– and pre–English A coursework to Harvard men, the documentation also reveals a group continually at odds with the criteria by which Harvard strove to create gentleman writers who took their education—and, more specifically, their literacy—seriously.

HARVARD'S COMMITTEE ON THE USE OF ENGLISH BY STUDENTS

On December 15, 1914, the Faculty of Arts and Sciences at Harvard University agreed to create the Committee on the Use of English by Students[6] in order to comply with a request from the Board of Governors (Committee on the Use of English by Students, "Nineteenth Annual Report," 1). The resolution from the board was as follows:

> In view of the various and convincing proofs brought to the attention of the Board of Governors that the students both in their entrance and college Examination papers, especially in courses other than English courses, fail to Write correct, coherent, and idiomatic English: *Resolved,* That the Faculty of Harvard College be requested to devise suitable measures to remedy this Condition of affairs, and to report to this Board not later than January 1, 1915, A definite plan for bettering the written and spoken English of Harvard students. (Committee on the Use, "Nineteenth Annual Report" 1)

The board reportedly drew its evidence from "hundreds of examination books, theses, and reports in a large number of courses" (Committee on the Use, "Report of the Committee" 1). From these, it was determined that "the writing of Harvard students is usually slip-shod, lacking in clearness and proper expressiveness, [and] lamentably weak in vocabulary. . . . [T]here is no concerted action among . . . the Faculty to raise the standard of English expression. . . . [As a result,] the students as a whole are not steadily made to feel that clearness and accuracy of expression are always important." Further, the board found that Harvard men "do not seriously try to express themselves well" especially given that "for a very large proportion of them the labor of producing good English is considerable and [determined to be not] worth while" (2). The board concluded that, in light of these problems, "some remedial action is clearly desirable" (1).

The response to this resolution and these charges of poor writing performance by Harvard men included the recommendations that (a) a "permanent" committee on the use of English by students be appointed, constituted by faculty of various departments; (b) the secretary of the committee be a faculty member and the "executive officer" whose duty will be to "inspect from time to time the written work of students, and to report to the Committee on its quality"; (c) "instructors in all departments, especially men recently appointed" discuss with the secretary "our students' usual faults and the best method of correcting them"; and (d) instructors "shall be expected" to refer "deficient" students to the secretary, who "may impose upon [these students] special tasks, such as outside reading and reports, or additional prescribed work in English composition, such work not counting for the degree" ("Report of the Committee" 2).

Just from this quick overview of the committee's structure and main charge, one can see both similarities to and divergences from Yale's Awkward Squad. As at Yale, students were remanded to the Committee's purview, but unlike the Awkward Squad, they were not put under the care of one lone instructor or tutor. Instead, they were officially registered with the Committee and became part of a codified, closed-door assistance plan for students deemed to be "deficient" in writing. Additionally, while in some ways the Harvard Committee's model may resemble an early version of a writing laboratory or center—with a specifically designated site for writing improvement existing outside the regular course structure—the committee's secretary was really the *only* instructor (rather than a group of tutors or instructors, as found in today's writing centers) *and* the secretary was free to assign "additional work" or "special tasks" in order to measure improvement in writing, unlike the typical writing center, which reviews and assists with only *existing*, externally assigned work. Finally, the Harvard Committee secretary was responsible for reading and responding to large quantities of student work *outside* of conference times, much like the load of a traditional classroom teacher. Dudley Hunt Cloud, secretary of the Committee during the late 1930s and early 1940s, writes that this individual responsibility to review all students' work involved reading "fifty to one hundred thousand words a week, [most of which was in] not very legible handwriting, [and] most deficient as English" ("Remedial English Work" 1). Moreover, cognizant of students' ignorance of audience in this type of task-centered work, even that which he himself has assigned, Cloud states, "[V]ery little of it has been especially written for me" ("Remedial English Work" 1).

Despite the labor-intensive duties of the secretary, the Committee was responsible for over forty years for overseeing the reporting and progress of students in need of additional writing instruction beyond English A. As proudly reported by the Committee in 1933, even though in this era it was "not an uncommon experience in colleges for interest in 'corrective English' to languish and die after two or three years," the committee through the 1930s—and forward into the 1940s and early 1950s—carried on a "vigorous campaign" to root out and remedy substandard English usage at Harvard.

The Committee was a tireless group that politely but persistently promoted its work to faculty, students, and administrators. The committee had a systematic approach for identifying and collecting students whose work in written English was below the standards of Harvard's faculty, both inside and outside the English department (see figs. 1 and 2). These collection cards were sent to all Harvard faculty in hopes that the Committee would be able to collect the names of men in need of its services. In particular, the cards were designed to facilitate quick and classifiable summaries of the men's difficulties, either in checklist (see fig. 1) or brief descriptive notation (see fig. 2). It is not clear from Committee records which instructors received which type of card; however, one may assume that faculty more likely to be descriptive and/or extensive in their remarks—for example, other English or writing teachers—may have received the open-response form, whereas faculty in other areas (or of other temperaments) may have preferred the checklist model. These cards, in both formats, were preaddressed and postmarked for easy mail return to the Committee's headquarters.

In addition to these postcards, the Committee sent out a series of memos and notices to both faculty and students asking for their participation in the Committee's work. These memos are striking for their appeals structure, which shifts slightly through the years of the Committee's work and in accordance with the number of students who were being reported for work in English F. The fewer

THE COMMITTEE ON THE USE OF ENGLISH BY STUDENTS

requests the name of any student whose grade in your course is seriously affected by misuse of English, or whose English falls below a standard that you would consider acceptable at Harvard.

STUDENT'S NAME CLASS

PLEASE CHECK THE STUDENT'S DEFICIENCIES ON THE FOLLOWING LIST:

Misspelling ....

Miswriting (omission of words or parts of words, transposition of letters, etc.) ....

Unidiomatic language ....

Incorrect usage ....

Faulty organization of material ....

Extreme wordiness ....

Faulty grammar ....

Incoherence in expressing thought ....

Faulty paragraphing ....

Faulty or overcomplicated sentence structure ....

COURSE .... SIGNATURE OF INSTRUCTOR ....

Fig. 1. Request card to Harvard faculty from the Committee on the Use of English by Students. Courtesy of the Harvard University Archives.

COMMITTEE ON THE USE OF ENGLISH BY STUDENTS

HARVARD UNIVERSITY

Please report students whose use of English is unsatisfactory in spelling or grammar, or in the clear expression of ideas.

CLASS	NAME	REMARKS

DATE____________________

COURSES____________________ SIGNATURE____________________

Fig. 2. Request card to Harvard faculty from the Committee on the Use of English by Students. Courtesy of the Harvard University Archives.

the number of students reported, the stronger was the rhetorical appeal made to faculty to find students in need of assistance. Despite how this may sound on the surface, the Committee was not promoting widespread reporting of students simply for the sake of numbers; in each of the archived memos, it is clear that the committee simply wishes to find *every* student in need of more writing instruction—lest it fail in its mission to eradicate the "most depressing exhibitions [of composition] which now confront us" ("Report of the Committee" 2).

The earliest available memo template is from January 1918. This memo clearly reflects the lack of response to the Committee's requests, in comparison to projected compliance:

> The Committee on the Use of English by Students is disappointed that only fifteen students have thus far been reported as writing unsatisfactorily. The Committee has reason to believe that there are many other men in Harvard College who need the help that the Secretary of the committee and the instructor in charge of English F could give. The Committee will be greatly obliged if you will report not only men who make absurd mistakes in spelling, punctuation, and the like, but also those who write just tolerably but might be taught to write really well, and those who are getting low marks because of their inability to arrange and express their ideas. (memo to Harvard Faculty, January 23, 1918)[7]

A few early principles of the Committee are evident from this memo. First, it sought aggressive and widespread reporting, based on the report of the board and, likely, anecdotal evidence of poorly written work received by faculty across the university. Second, the Committee believed that its charge was *not* simply to fix grammatical errors or "clean up" what it deemed "absurd" errors in writing. Instead, it valued improvement in organization and style and wanted not only the very *worst* writers but also those who resided somewhere in the middle—put somewhat indelicately as those who "write just tolerably." This is a slight departure from the original mandate, which expressed need for "remediation"—not exactly the work required in teaching decent writers to become excellent writers. Nonetheless, by expanding their student base to include not just obviously underprepared writers but also occasionally struggling ones, the Committee would increase its numbers and its visibility as the arm of the campus that publicly and forcefully sought to bring Harvard men "up to standards" set by the institution.

In May 1922, another template for a faculty memo is created, this time signed by T. L. Hood, one of the early secretaries of the Committee and a vocal supporter of its mission. This memo is notable for its added information about the work of the committee—including statistics on students—and its more nuanced rhetorical stance toward culling faculty compliance in reporting students for work in English F. Addressed specifically to faculty who did not send reports to the Committee at the "midyear period," the memo relays that these faculty

> will find it convenient to send to the Secretary, in the envelope enclosed herewith, a report in the usual form. It may be prepared in the course of reading a group of theses or examinations, by checking on a class list the names of men whose writing appears to need attention, distinguishing the worst cases with asterisks. Such reports most frequently include the names of about ten percent of the students in a course. The Committee would like to have every class or section of a class equally represented in the reports on which it depends for the selection of students who most need assistance in writing. There is no danger of reporting too many, and no possible bad result from even a large amount of uncertainty in the reports. . . . The Committee will not divulge to any student the names of the courses from which he has been reported. (Hood)

This memo is remarkably persuasive in two respects. First, it clearly suggests to faculty a "standard" number of students to report to the Committee (10 percent), providing both a benchmark for reporting as well as a logical presumption of authority in its charge—that it is regularly serving 10 percent of all Harvard men. Second, the memo provides assurance of *confidentiality*, something that may seem unnecessary on the surface but which may point to a deeper concern among the faculty, leading to a compliance issue where the Committee is concerned. If faculty were both hesitant to "overreport" men or suspicious that such work was not needed of the typical Harvard student, perhaps they were also concerned about the repercussions of reporting men of particular standing in the college?[8]

In 1925, the memo template again changes, this time providing more information about the specific work done in English F:

> [T]he work is adjusted to each individual student. Diction, punctuation, spelling, and the correct construction of sentences receive much attention; there is also a great deal of work in connection with methods of reading, taking notes, writing tests and examinations, analyzing subjects, organizing and preparing reports and theses, and the development of varied and expressive style. The Committee therefore hopes that reports may include the names not only of the men obviously deficient in elementary matters, but of all men who belong to the larger group that English F is designed to serve. (Memo to Harvard Faculty, November 4, 1925)

Here one sees the notable appeal to send not just "remedial" students but also students belonging to the amorphous "larger group" of would-be English F patrons to the Committee. This strategy is laid bare in subsequent years' memos, for example, the 1932 sample, which asks that faculty point the Committee "toward those students who can not or *will not* write satisfactory English in examinations, although they are apparently able to do so in other college exercises" (McMullen, April 1, 1932). By appealing to the perceived common course denominator of poorly written essay-exam responses—an original concern of the 1914 board proclamation—the Committee hoped to "recruit" a significant group of students from these instructors' courses.

In 1936—one of the last years for which the Committee's regular, faculty memos are archived—the appeal structure begins to sound quite literally like a pledge drive, especially in its closing request, which politely yet firmly reminds faculty of their institutional duty to send their students to the Committee, even if their predecessors have been less conscientious in doing so. It additionally employs new data connecting overall student success and their status with the Committee:

> Each year for the past seven years approximately five per cent of our undergraduate students were reported [to the Committee]. Whether or not this percentage represents an irreducible minimum the Committee has no way of determining. Some indication one way or another would be had if all instructors would be especially vigilant during the present college year. . . . Evidence of the intimate relation between ability to write and academic standing is to be seen in the fact that of the 112 students reported at mid-term last year, 38 were entered at that time in the College Records Office as "unsatisfactory." May the Committee count on your cooperation in the work of discovering the students, both undergraduate and graduate, who need further instruction in writing? (McMullen, October 21, 1936)

In December 1942, as World War II progressed and servicemen filled the ranks of American colleges, Secretary Stanley Salmen of the Committee put out a special memo appealing to faculty who taught these "special" students at Harvard, with particular attention paid to the hopelessness some of these faculty may have felt in teaching an increasingly unfamiliar kind of Harvard student, alongside past elite admits and in the face of the country's overall lessened attention to the gentleman's language standards of the nineteenth century:

> Many students would be more aware of the value of good English composition, even in wartime, if they realized that satisfactory written expression is one of the basic requirements for officer candidates for both the Army and Navy. . . . Many instructors now feel, apparently, that nothing can be done about bad English at this late date, or hold the optimistic impression that the student understands the facts of the subject, whether or not he is able to express them. The experience of this committee proves that, without exception, a student can

> improve the quality of his composition if he really wants to. The way to make him improve his writing is to insist that he must. (memo to Harvard Faculty, December 4, 1942)

This memo's central plea is clear: Don't give up, and don't feel that any one student (or type of student) cannot—or should not—benefit from the work of the Committee or English F.

The number of students reported to the Committee varied from year to year and included both the men remanded for additional work as well as men who elected to work with the Committee in order to improve their writing; this included undergraduate as well as a small number of graduate students. Based on available Committee reports, table 2 provides an overall sense of how many students were served by the Committee between 1914 and 1942.

This lingering question of whom to report, for what reasons, and how often is addressed head-on in the twenty-third annual report of the Committee, issued in 1938 and focusing on the performance of the Class of 1936. This report states that over the past five years (1933 to 1938), on average, 175 students had been reported to the Committee annually. However, the report makes clear, "This figure . . . does *not*, however, represent the number of undergraduate students in the College in any one of the past five years who were unable to write satisfactory English" (1). Comparing the average of 21 percent of the total college enrollment being reported to the Committee, as figured from the annual reports, to this minor 1938 figure of 5 percent being reported, the report is clearly pessimistic about the actual number of needy students who are receiving help from the Committee, projecting that many seniors who have been unreported will finally be reported just prior to graduation, swelling the ranks of the reported to closer to 10 percent but at a point almost too late to be of help (1). The report estimates that in 1938, despite the 175 students reported, Harvard actually had "329 students . . . who are unable to write satisfactory English" (2).

But the 1938 report does not simply tackle the faculty's compliance with the Committee's reporting requests; it also addresses, quite explicitly, what type of students have been reported to the committee—specifically students from preparatory academies versus

Table 2.
Number and percentage of Harvard University students served by the Committee, 1916–42

Year of instruction	Number of students served by the Committee[1]		Percentage of students served to total Harvard University students[2] (%)
	Reported	Instructed	
1916	235		8
1917	177		5
1918	83		10
1922	501	196	17
1923	404	214	12
1929	235	143	7.5
1930	193	129	6
1933	144		7
1934	174		5
1935	204		n/a
1936	176		n/a
1937	153		n/a
1938	156		n/a
1939	193		n/a
1942	167		n/a

SOURCES: Annual reports, Committee on the Use of English by Students, Harvard University.
NOTES: 1. In some annual reports, the statistics compare students reported to students instructed. Not all of the reports made this distinction; hence, the missing data in some years listed.
2. The Committee's nineteenth annual report, 1934, includes a table of the total percentage of students reported to the Committee between 1916 and 1933; hence, the missing data in some years listed. I have matched the percentages to the whole number reports from the other available years to create this chart.

so-called second-rate high schools (2). In doing so, this annual report exposes a fear also raised by admissions officials at Yale in the late 1950s—that students from the "best" schools in the country were actually frequently the worst prepared (as well as the worst-behaved segment of students on campus). The 1938 Committee report charts ten of the top feeder, preparatory schools from which Harvard admitted students into the Class of 1936. Of these ten schools, including Andover, Exeter, and Groton, among others, 274 students were admitted, and 77 of those students were reported to the Committee for work in English F. The report notes that while "students from [these schools] accounted for 44% of the students reported . . . admissions from these ten schools comprised only 25% of the freshman enrollment" (2). Additionally, in the annual Committee report of 1942, it is noted that while 57 percent of the students enrolled at Harvard during this year (including freshmen, sophomores, juniors, and seniors) came from private/preparatory schools, 91 of those 167 men reported to the Committee, or 54.5 percent, were from these schools. Thus, the makeup of the students doing work with the Committee during this year almost exactly reflected the proportional admissions of the Harvard student population at large.

Such statistics turn a magnifying lens on the false assumptions that faculty, students, and staff may have had toward the preparedness of the *most* "elite" students at Harvard—those emerging from privileged locations including high-priced, exclusive boarding and preparatory schools. That a full 25 percent to 50 percent of those students themselves asked to enroll in English F were from this elite population is further telling evidence that so-called remedial instruction, even at Harvard, was not limited to the disadvantaged or conditionally admitted students of the incoming class nor those from the wider frontier of the western United States, as implied in the Yale archival documents. Here was clear evidence that, from a historical standpoint, English F was significantly serving Harvard's own—its privileged, eastern-seaboard students, who were likely one of many in their families who had attended the institution. And these students, perhaps above all others, were bound to be the type of Harvard gentlemen whom the institution was designed to produce.

As a result, while the 1938 report laments these statistics regarding English F students who were admitted from preparatory schools, the Committee agreed, "Means for co-operating with these preparatory schools could readily be devised, but before anything is attempted, we should put our own house in order" (3). In a sense, Harvard was fighting its own admissions legacy, which theoretically cultivated these student-types as their target populace but which in practice revealed these students' social location to be a false indication of ability, as they were socially "relocated" to remedial writing courses more often than not within the Harvard curriculum.

As further evidenced from an extensive scrapbook kept by the Committee documenting correspondence and other memorabilia between 1917 and 1935, this desire to keep a "tidy house"[9] was both admired and emulated by other colleges and universities around the country. Unlike Yale's rather secretive approach to remedial writing instruction, Harvard's approach was disseminated widely, perhaps in large part via its alumni correspondence and academic-related communications. Documenting this public knowledge are letters from chairs, writing directors, and deans at sixteen institutions found in the Committee's scrapbook—including correspondence from other elite schools such as Princeton, Emory, Northwestern, and Smith; state land-grant schools such as Indiana, Illinois, Wisconsin, and Ohio State; and smaller private colleges such as Knox and Washington and Jefferson. These letters either sing the praises of the Committee's work, ask for information that would help them start a similar program at their own institutions, or, most often, both. For example, a November 16, 1919, letter from Frank N. Scott, an English professor who was clearly a drafted rather than volunteer participant in remedial instruction at the University of Illinois, explains,

> I am the goat on whom or which the work of installing a Committee on Students' English has been unloaded for the present year, and I am naturally turning to the source of all light in things English for some guidance. Our plan is based on that used at Harvard, and includes the privilege of holding up a man at any station in his career for further work in English

> composition. . . . If you can tell me, or ask anyone there to tell me, how the work of your committee of this nature has progressed, I shall be very grateful indeed.

Similarly, H. P. Miller, chairman of freshman composition at Emory, writes on May 3, 1930:

> The English Department of Emory University is seeking to find some effective means of sustaining a high standard of writing for all students throughout their entire time in college. It seems that students who barely pass a course in freshman composition very quickly begin to slip back into their former incorrect writing habits. Unless some further attention is given . . . their writing will soon become inferior to a decent standard for college men. The English Department of Emory University is seeking some effective means of preventing this laxity in writing. The Department would like to know what, if any, specific means your department uses to enforce better writing after a student has passed a required course in freshman composition.

And, from Henry Adelbert White, professor at Washington and Jefferson College, made a more familiar request, made on November 6, 1922, as a Harvard alumnus and as a faculty member:

> The *Harvard Alumni Weekly* mentions a statement just made covering the work that you are doing to improve the writing and speaking of Harvard students beyond what the ordinary classes can accomplish. I wonder if it would be possible to send us a more definite statement of the report and the conditions you have to try to modify or correct. In years past I have had some information of this kind from Harvard, where I was a graduate student once, and it has been of good service to us here. . . . Harvard can assist us all over America by taking a very energetic lead in matters of English. It might not be a bad idea to refuse a diploma now and then on the ground that the student does not know his own language![10]

These letters, as well as others found in the scrapbook, demonstrate a few historical truths about remedial English and Harvard as an institution during this time period. First, the Committee's work was widely known, due not just to alumni bulletins but also, given the social strata and gender of most academics during this era, to the fact that many professors at other colleges were likely to be Harvard graduates or to be acquainted with Harvard men. Second, the Committee's work was clearly looked to as a model for other institutions and a model that was *post*admission (rather than at the entrance/placement level) in its design. Third, even though many elite institutions today, by and large, are still loathe to associate themselves with "remediation," Harvard's Committee proudly shared their working ideas on the subject with other colleges and universities. This last point about publicity is critical, as Harvard's Committee actively sought to recast their work as something better than "remedial" and closer to "corrective" in nature. In other words, the problem is not hopeless or a matter of permanent identity—it is *fixable*, and that "fixing" can come at any time, so long as it occurs before the man graduates. This attitude—though born of a desire to promote the perfect picture of the Harvard man—contrasts sharply with the regard for underprepared students today, who are frequently seen as lepers wandering the halls of their institutions, draining resources via their "subcollege" presentations in writing classrooms. In other words, while remedial writers at Harvard during the first half of the twentieth century were down, they were clearly not *out*. Rather, the Committee, as a historical public entity, served as a source of refinement, for some a site of individual "finishing," fulfilling a higher social and communal purpose that most faculty and students agreed was vital, if sometimes inconvenient, for Harvard men to endure.

BUILDING THE PERFECT GENTLEMAN (WRITER) AT HARVARD UNIVERSITY

As David Jolliffe has observed about the themes of men enrolled in English A at Harvard at the turn of the century, the topics for writing in this course "suggest . . . an invitation, if not a mandate, for students to observe the manners of the world and to turn from their observations to the task of shaping their fellow beings' moral behavior" (164). Jolliffe argues that the "cultural and social context taught the Harvard men that their themes were exercises in cultural criticism and, as pieces of art, must have a moral dimension . . . reflect[ing] the idea of a 'moral aesthetic' incorporated in rhetorical and belletristic education by such influential pedagogical authorities as Hugh Blair but prevalent generally in English and American society" (170). As is apparent in the 1914 Committee report, Harvard's faculty and administrators still looked to England for its portrait of the ideal man and set this ideal in political motion by invoking an explicit comparison between the boys of England and the boys of Harvard in designing goals for acceptable English composition at Harvard.

But as L. B. R. Briggs had argued back in 1890, "We are prone to forget that English grammar is not training in knowledge, but the far higher training in judgment" (36), which is often difficult for beginning college students, given that in a timed entrance exam, "it is unreasonable to ask an excited boy, with a meager allowance of time, to fashion a symmetrical organism out of a tangle of arms and legs" (33). For Briggs, a student's ability (or inability) to correct "bad English" on the entrance examinations was, thus, not always a fair marker of what that student can do in a more extended, thoughtful, classroom setting. His view may be paraphrased as thus: it is not that a boy is not *capable* of such an ideal; it is that he is not put into the right *conditions* to exhibit this capability. Such forward-thinking views toward writing and revision would be both embraced at the level of instruction and ignored at the level of program execution and faculty appeals in the rush to gain clientele for the English F course.

This tension between an ideal, England-rooted aesthetic and its real-world impediments continued into the twentieth century in Harvard's composition courses. Such a view also significantly influenced the way in which students were not only mandated to basic writing courses but also the impulse to *perfect* student skills before graduation. During the first half of the twentieth century, it was not enough to complete requirements in writing and move on; the student must excel at this (and every subject) in order to be a true Harvard man. Harvard men were groomed to be leaders—not simply observers but commentators and policymakers, the best of the best that American education could or would produce. Such a belief carried on the tradition voiced by Charles William Eliot, president of Harvard in the mid- to late nineteenth century, who said that while Harvard would "support poor students of capacity" these students must also be "of promising ability and best character" (qtd. in H. P. Miller 51). This aim for substance in college writing that reflects such "ability and character," even when pushed to the aesthetic extreme, is not necessarily a bad impulse; modern composition and rhetoric courses also impart this type of pedagogy in the format of a variety of libratory and cultural studies–based pedagogies. In short, we do not—and should not—ask students to write just for the sake of writing, nor should we necessarily remain completely neutral about the kind of students we are producing as a result of our assignments and curricula. But at an elite location such as Harvard, this desire to make men—however selectively chosen—into leaders, in no small part through their writing, heavily influenced how much and how often additional (and frequently remediated) writing instruction was required of students post–English A.

In his contribution to the 1929 collection *Harvard Professors Write about Their Own Departments*, Professor John Strong Perry Tatlock broadly describes the English composition courses and the rationale behind it in place at Harvard during the 1920s:

> The first group of courses includes those in English Composition, of which there are many, adapted to students of all degrees of maturity and proficiency. Inasmuch as writing is an art, which means doing rather than knowing, and as the function of a university is primarily to teach knowledge, no student is permitted to offer for the degree an unlimited number of these courses. But nearly all of the other courses require such an individual reaction to what has been learned, and such self-expression, as is involved by writing about it. (19)

Tatlock's comments evidence the competing perspectives at work in the standard and remedial course offerings in Harvard's composition program prior to 1960. There exists a clear attention to "all degrees of maturity and proficiency," as opposed to the one-size-fits-all (or not) approach prevalent at institutions such as Yale during this time. Such an apparently inclusive principle is evident ten years prior to Tatlock's writings. The 1918–19 Harvard *Courses of Instruction* describes the composition curriculum as that which is "directly adapted to individual needs and interests in composition, either in connection with the written work of other courses or independent of immediate college writing requirements."

This need to adapt to student ability and interest is reinforced—and complicated, from a social perspective—by Samuel Eliot Morison in *The Development of Harvard University since the Inauguration of President Eliot, 1869–1929*. Morison notes, when discussing the English department's offerings:

> Special provision has been made for those who in their College courses seem unable to write with passable correctness. We have now had for several years a Committee on the Use of English, with a Secretary who takes in hand the pupils reported to him by teachers in various departments, gives them fatherly advice, and sees to it that they receive the steering that should be theirs. (170)

Morison's description of the committee's duties, including the critical charge of giving "fatherly advice" to students in need of extra writing instruction, is critical in interpreting the position and function of remedial writing at Harvard in the first half of the twentieth century. Certainly, the range of courses targeting different levels of ability, as well as different desires for improvement, exhibits a liberal approach to writing instruction and, importantly, writing *improvement*—beyond a basic requirement that was to be satisfied and forgotten. But the impetus for this improvement was more than just intellectual; it was social, representational, in its approach. Harvard men, simply put, must be the best writers that a college can produce.

But how did Harvard students respond to these lofty ideals and the strict promotion of perfection by not only their instructors but the Committee on the Use of English and its concomitant courses? Certainly, Harvard students had a history of being vocal about their

English requirements, as evidenced by the "Petition against Military English" drafted in 1918, in response to the department's proposal to teach this specialized discourse in its lower-division courses in order to comply with government recommendations for undergraduate enlisted men. The *Harvard Crimson*, the student publication of Harvard University and the source of a variety of editorials about the English A–F requirements, published an article in May 1951 opining that whether a student requires "a half hour 'pep talk' [or] years of non-credit English work," students who demonstrate work "below a standard . . . acceptable at Harvard" must be brought to those standards ("Committee Goes After Men Misusing English on Exams").

A 1923 *Crimson* piece on English F argues similarly that the course of "special instruction" was for students deemed to have "faulty" use of English, but those men who are "really deficient in the use of English . . . should never have been admitted to Harvard, [since] 'the well educated man,' President Eliot once said, 'is the man who knows how to use his own language well.'" The article concludes by maintaining that there is "little excuse for [English F's] existence except as an elective course for foreign students." The (uncredited) student author of this article asserts, "If [a student] has been admitted to Harvard and has passed his English A requirement, it must be humiliating to the pride of the college to feel that he is in need of English F" ("English F").

Keep in mind that these are *student* perspectives being voiced about *fellow students*. The trickle-down parroting of "high standards" rhetoric from administrators to faculty to students is impossible to ignore in the context of any remedial or supplemental writing curriculum offered during this era. The students being placed into English F were also skeptical of its use value, as evident in the cartoon (see fig. 3) from the *Harvard Lampoon*, published sometime prior to 1930, likely in the mid-1920s.[11] This cartoon obviously expresses some of the resistance among students to the English F course. These students, emerging from their offices at the *Harvard Crimson*, are joking about being remanded to Course F, despite their status as writers (or editors) of this successful and prestigious college newspaper. Such an attitude should not be unfamiliar to those who have heard complaints from students who, having received accolades for their writing in other settings (high school, nonacademic groups, even writing-intensive courses within the institution) are then placed into—or remanded to—basic composition courses.

Nonetheless, the Committee kept its spirits up about such men, at least in public correspondence. In 1939, Secretary Cloud responds

"Never mind those eds. fellows. We'll be late for English F."

Fig. 3. English F cartoon, *Harvard Lampoon,* ca. 1920–30. Courtesy of the Harvard University Archives.

to a query about students' compliance with the Committee's work: "One or two students in this past year have been so angry at being reported that I had trouble getting them to admit any defects in their writing. . . . [But] the largest group of all [reported to the Committee] is composed of men who are disturbed at being reported, and who are ambitious to improve: for these men there is hope" (letter to Jerome Greene, 29 June 1939). Occasionally, student attitudes toward the course that were less positive also surfaced in Committee interviews and commentary. In a March 1932 issue of the *Crimson*, Secretary A. J. McMullen explained that even though most students realize that "English F . . . is a help and not a penalty," there was still some variability in student reaction to the Committee's work:

> When a man is sent to us for extra help, he takes one of three attitudes. He may be openly hostile, and come banging his way in; . . . he may be curious as to what [the Committee's work] is all about, and just what English F is; or he may be one of those excused from English A, and hence is amused that he, of all people, should be thought insufficiently well-trained in his mother tongue. (qtd. in "Students Apt")

The notion that students may be "amused" is clearly depicted in the *Harvard Lampoon* cartoon (see fig. 3) and also present in Carroll Towle's description of Awkward Squad students at Yale (see chap. 4). This "amusement" was, apparently, a face-saving mechanism common among otherwise privileged and socially successful elite students suddenly faced with the prospect of remediation.

The *Crimson* ran regular, brief pieces on the progress of the Committee, as well as the content and scope of the English A–F curricula, keeping students abreast of any changes in requirements. Typically, these articles were curricular updates, such as the announcement of the change from English A to the General Education program in 1949, the enrollment of multiple student "volunteers" in English F in 1930, and the focus on reviewing the writing done in exams as a primary goal for the Committee and English F tutorials. Sometimes, however, the newspaper voiced the frustration of students with the writing curricula in a less-than-objective manner. After calling the English A course instruction in "the fundamentals of writing through overcrowded sections and dull weekly themes," the *Crimson* reported in February 1949 that "the College's largest and most sadly over-extended course is up for a complete and thorough revision" ("New Look for English A"). In a May 1951 piece, a student writer disparages the post–English A work done by the Committee:

> Faulty paragraphing or a brace of misspelled words on a final exam this week may bring the wrath of the committee down upon the head of some unsuspecting Social Relations man. Indeed, so broad are the powers of this little-publicized group that it can hold up a student's degree if it deems his use of English unsatisfactory. ("Committee Goes")

This same piece also notes that in the late 1930s (in fact, in 1939, though this year is not cited in the piece), the Committee "made available of all the essays written for a History 1 mid-year exam. . . . Newspapers all over the country seized upon the bad essay, ignored the good one altogether, and published editorials exposing "the way American college students write today."

Both of these student writer comments show an exasperation with the work of the Committee, both locally—as it "goes after" Harvard men for the slightest linguistic infraction—and nationally as it provides newspaper fodder linking Harvard students to poor writing. The prominent position of the committee among other institutions, in this manner, is perceived as a clear negative to students who clearly feel their writing is in no need of "fixing." The late date of these editorials is also in fairly clear contrast to the earlier reporting of the *Crimson* on "unsatisfactory" use of English among Harvard men. In earlier years of the Committee's work, the *Crimson* had found it alarming that such poor usage existed; now, after thirty-plus years of seeing students reported to English C, D, and F and after moving to a general-education curriculum, the newspaper seems to have grown weary of the oversight function the Committee occupies.

Indeed, the letters from the Committee that students received asking them to report to Warren House for testing, evaluation, and instruction, were wide ranging in their tone and rationale. A sample student memo from December 1925 evidences a soft-sell approach in the earlier years of the Committee's existence, a courteous appeal to the "gentleman" at the heart of the student being called in for further assistance:

> The Committee on the Use of English by Students desires to inform you that the English in some of your written work has been reported as apparently below the general standard. Since you have not been reported before, and since the writing on which the report was based may not have been fairly representative of your work, the Committee wishes at this time merely to direct your attention to the requirement that the written work in all courses should be reasonably correct, coherent, and idiomatic. If you feel that it would be to your advantage to consider, and perhaps to improve, the quality of your writing in tests, reports, theses, or examinations, you may readily secure advice and assistance. . . . The work begins and ends entirely at the pleasure of the student, at any time during the college year. . . . Please call on the Secretary of the Committee at Warren House 24 whenever you deem it advisable to do so. (English F student memo, December 18, 1925)

Comparatively, a sample student memo from February 24, 1942, takes a more stringent, authoritarian approach when communicating about the student's need for remedial work and comes from the secretary of the Committee (at this time, Cloud):

> According to my records, you have not completed the requirement of English D. You must complete this requirement during this year or you will face disciplinary action next year for not doing so . Remember that I want to see every exercise you write in English this year. In the next week or so, please bring to my office whatever papers you have collected for me. (English D student memo)

Some of the difference in tone between these two sample memos is due to the difference in how the Committee viewed and subsequently promoted the freestanding English F tutorial and the more punitive, mandatory English D course. Students who were remanded to English D or its earlier course counterpart(s) were expected to complete this course and were not allowed to opt out of it prior to graduation. In contrast, students recommended for English F were both the product of faculty referrals as well as students who sought out the Committee's help without any faculty recommendation. English F was thus the more fluid and more progressive of the two remedial assistance options at Harvard. At the same time, as the Committee's work progressed through the 1940s and began to take on more responsibilities for remedial instruction with less faculty support, its correspondences with both students and faculty took on a more urgent tone. After the Committee was asked to head up the work of not only English F but also English D in 1941, its secretary became increasingly put-upon to serve as the sole savior of students with poor communication skills. Add to this the pressures of a student body that was perhaps beginning to resist the Committee's work more as it looked to the promises of the more free-ranging general-education plan, and one can see a subtle shift from assistive to punitive in these back-and-forth communications. Such memos offer a preview of the difficulties that basic writing programs, as well as writing tutorials, face today on many campuses but especially campuses where students (and supporting faculty) share educational and social experiences that discount or contradict the notion that they, too, could benefit from additional writing instruction.

Taking this history of Harvard's remedial curricula into account, my final chapter turns to the present and future of basic writing students and programs—the continued resistance, the inevitable rejection, the gross marginalization—and addresses the age-old question to which this archival evidence, suggesting the importance of locating remedial writing in an institutional context, invariably leads:

What do we do now?

6

Looking Forward, Looking Back: Locating Basic Writing Today

> We are introducing a remedial English program for the first time next year. In recent travels, I have talked to people at Harvard, Yale, Stanford, etc. who are also recognizing the need for remedial English even at the best schools. Why not have a conference on the topic, "Remedial English for the *Advantaged* Student"?
>
> —Joseph Williams, University of Chicago,
> *ADE Bulletin*, September 1975

AS EVIDENCED IN THE PREVIOUS CHAPTERS of this book, basic writing students are not now nor have they historically been confined to one type of educational location. With the advent of online learning, the rapid growth in the number of transfer students, and the increased pressure in today's job economy not just to attend college but to attend an *elite* college, basic writers are even less likely to further filter into one academic location. Thus, basic writing studies must be cognizant of its disparate social histories and willing to advocate for writers from elite as well as non-elite backgrounds and institutions. We thus must not isolate basic writers at elite colleges from the larger discussions taking place regarding first-year writing curricula but instead consider their histories and futures in the complicated, often frustrating context of what it means for a student to come to write in college. Further, we need to think about the longitudinal future of composition as a course and a discipline, in particular whether the subdivisions of the first-year writing program do a true service to the field's mission of educating and producing competent, inquisitive writers for the university setting and beyond.

Some scholars in composition have begun to question the declared attributes of "college-level writing"—a fluid and inevitably unstable definition that if lacking uniformity and purpose is followed by the further, imminent collapse of what "basic writing" means as a prerequisite for it. These conversations about standards are usually situated as questions of articulation—between community colleges and four-year institutions or between high-school and college writing programs. The pressing question is this: If we cannot decide what "college-level" work is, then is it not impossible to further demarcate what so-called precollege or basic work is? This is a problem that has long gone unsolved, perhaps because writing programs (and their faculty) generally agree that there is *some* definition—elusive and evolving though it may be. (Or, as the saying goes, "I know it when I see it.") There is also an agreement that students *need* some sort of "college-level" writing instruction—even if such needs vary from institution to institution.

Now, as governmental initiatives such as the Spellings Report, fueled by the lingering desire to fully integrate and thereby standardize the K-16 educational experience, loom large outside the doors of college writing programs and control and severely limit writing instruction at the secondary level as well, we are compelled to address this problem as one of *assessment*—how can we articulate common goals? How can we provide students, parents, and the faculty teaching these courses with clear learning objectives and student outcomes? In leaning on the vocabulary of assessment to indirectly answer the question of what is college-level, however, we sidestep the question of what *defines* such writing or, more pertinent to this book, what makes it superior to or more desirable than "basic" writing.[1]

This final chapter brings together the threads of my argument regarding definitions and labels for basic writing by briefly examining the larger ramifications of the fluid definitions of *basic* in the context of today's writing programs. I am specifically interested in how these fluid definitions both complicate and stand to reify the ways in which we position the first-year writers coming into our institutions and the first-year writing courses that lead into their other university experiences. I posit an erasure of the label of *basic* altogether in favor of the broader category of *introductory*—a category that would encompass *all* versions of first-year writing at the college level, not just the first or lowest course in the sequence, thus eliminating the designation of remedial/basic/"precollege" courses within the curriculum. Such a category need not even result in an official on-the-ground course label, depending upon institutional choice, yet would better suit the changing demands and political realities of college writing instruction and level the differences among students moving between and among different colleges and universities, each with differing values and expectations. Such a leveling of terms, rather than a standardizing of values or expectations, would serve as a symbolic step toward addressing the warring conceptions of "college-level" designations in first-year writing curricula today.

(RE)DEFINING A DEFINITION: COLLEGE-LEVEL VERSUS "PRECOLLEGE" WRITING

Patrick Sullivan and Howard Tinberg's 2006 collection *What Is "College Level" Writing?* serves as a useful starting place for this query into the fluidity of curricular parameters, as the book adeptly answers the question posed in its title by providing multiple, diverse responses—none of which lay claim to one agreed-upon or "standard" way to define what college level is. Sullivan and Tinberg's book does more to expose the contradictions underlying the term *college level* than to define it within the nation's postsecondary curriculum. Such productive dissent is the purpose of their collection, which speaks directly to the arguments I've made in this book regarding the ever-present fluid parameters for "basic" in local, historical contexts.

In his introductory chapter, Patrick Sullivan argues that, given how divergent faculty can be when discussing issues of definition,

> it may very well be that [such] conflicts are irresolvable and that all standards related to our students' written work must ultimately be local, determined at least in part by our response to the complex realities of the communities we serve and the individuals we teach. Any discussion of shared standards may require us to ignore or discount the very powerful political

> and social realities that shape students' lives on individual campuses and in particular learning communities. We must also acknowledge that much outstanding scholarly work has already been done to address this issue, especially in the area of basic writing. On the other hand, it may well be that our profession could enormously benefit from reopening a dialogue about this question. (2–3)

I believe that Sullivan is right on the mark in his call to reconsider writing standards in local, political, social contexts but that he is overly hopeful in asserting that much "has already been done" toward this reconsideration—at least where basic writing is concerned. Indeed, even as basic writing programs have emerged and have allowed students to intellectually thrive *because* these programs refuse to allow the standards for first-year writing admission or placement or exemption to dismiss their abilities and potentials, we could, as a discipline, be much more inclusive in terms of our assistance for such writers if were we to eliminate the notion of "basic" altogether.

Sullivan and Tinberg showcase some powerful arguments for reconsidering what "standard" composition means—a critical starting point, I believe, for further reconsidering the levels and differentiations put upon students in first-year writing programs. Again, I do not argue that we should sidestep or stand in ignorance of writers whose needs are greater than others in our college communities; rather, I argue that *calling* these writers something "special"—even if that label is accommodating, welcoming, or generous in spirit—connotes a historical baggage that Mina Shaughnessy attempted to diminish but instead reified as a label only available to some and not others within first-year writing programs. Considering some of the individual arguments set forth in Sullivan and Tinberg's collection provides a sample blueprint for how (and why) we might work toward doing away with such ability definitions altogether.

For starters, we need to return to the high-school writing program or rather the typical series of literature-based English courses and the perspective of students who emerge from it. The tension between high-school and college writing courses and programs is historical and ongoing, with neither camp truly understanding or pedagogically undertaking the perspective of the other. Recent moves toward bringing together high-school and college writing teachers show great promise. But we cannot forget—especially those of us who work in graduate programs and who thus infrequently see the inside of a first-year classroom, let alone a junior- or senior-level high-school classroom—that misconceptions still exist about what the differences are or should be between high-school and college writing.

Putting aside for a moment the well-known logistical and pedagogical problems this divide creates for writing faculty, we must first acknowledge the students' perspective in transitioning to college-level writing, as succinctly stated by Milka Mustenikova Mosley, a Georgia high-school English teacher, in "The Truth about High School English":

> High school level writing is usually very predictable. High school students typically write mainly to conform. They want to know exactly how many words they need to write, when the assignment is due, and whether or not they need to say "I" in their piece. Occasionally they will . . . try to incorporate new vocabulary into their essays, but oftentimes these words do not work well within the context of their essays. This is due to their lack of reading and writing expectations, to their youthfulness and age, and to already established routines. All they have done since kindergarten has been conforming to the requirements set before them by their educators. (59)

There are familiar, yet critical reminders here regarding students' willingness to "follow along" within the curriculum and seek confirmation of their good behavior, something that clearly impacts upon how they respond to high-stakes measures of their writing futures at the university. We have all seen the laudatory representation of the five-paragraph theme in even the so-called best incoming college students and have lamented these students' clear inability—at a physical, task-oriented level—to break out of this convenient yet limited structure in order to express their ideas and beliefs in writing. But the student perspective on such tried-and-true structural templates is something we can forget when we ask students to meet the more lofty organizational and even rebellious expectations in our individual college writing programs—local demands that, in truth, vary far more widely than do the highly standardized high-school curricula, thanks to No Child Left Behind and other similar state-level mandates. In this regard, Mosley reminds us that despite the best intentions taught to candidates in teacher-education programs and even graduate programs in composition and rhetoric, "college theory and high school practice differ greatly," even in advanced placement– or precollege-track classrooms, where students still lack confidence in their own language abilities and where teachers are limited to prescribed curricular goals and activities, including delivering a mainly literature-based reading and writing program (60, 63).

This lack of confidence stems from both a vague knowledge of what is to come in the college setting (perhaps from friends already enrolled, or counselors who provide college pamphlets and the like, or brief campus visits crammed with program information) and a fearful realization that any requirements for writing will still be beyond anything the student can hope to prepare for preadmissions, even within advanced coursework. In this context, I find Mosley's distinction between *youthfulness* and *age* a telling one when considering how entry-level writing courses are constructed and then subdivided into designations of standard and basic. I do believe that there is a true and present perspective of *youthfulness*, as Mosley notes, in first-year students and, ergo, in first-year student writing. This perspective, as noted above, is not just due to a student's age; indeed, one can find in any given class an eighteen-year-old whose life and literacy experiences are anything but "youthful." Similarly, there are twenty-three-year-old seniors or even older students on occasion whose perspective is still "youthful" due to their own inexperience with writing and literacy. To be "youthful" is to be unaware, perhaps, or to be uncompromised by the pressures of college literacy and the looming world of work—the threat held over students' heads on a regular basis in these high-assessment, economically driven times. To be youthful is also to be open to change, experiment, direction, sometimes ignorant of the real and psychic costs of that change.

On the other hand, "youthful" in Mosley's analysis also means *inexperience*—ignorance of conventions and standards that are widespread and will mark the student as adequate or failing. Reflecting upon my own basic writing classes, many students I have encountered have been allowed (by teachers, parents, and/or peers) to avoid any compromises or conflicts in their own education, resulting in a kind of youthfulness that, ultimately, does them a great disservice upon admission to the university. This sense of "youthful" thus characterizes many a basic writing student on our college campuses but also many a "standard" college writing enrollee as well. Herein lies the matter of degree—of valuation, calculation, discretionary judgment—that creates the great dividing line between these two groups of writers.

Lynn Z. Bloom interrogates the ways in which these grading judgments are made, based on college writing teachers' willingness to cultivate not just "good" work but also "good enough" work in their courses and in their larger assessments of student competencies. In Bloom's argument, writing teachers are all too willing to accept a kind of mediocrity, a level of performance that meets standards, particularly those ascribed to larger social behaviors, because that is the underlying structure of the evaluative system in higher education:

> Good enough writing is characterized by a clutch of Academic Virtues. These include *Rationality; Conformity, Conventionality*—which is attained by using Standard English, following the rules, and otherwise maintaining proper academic decorum; *Self Reliance, Responsibility, Honesty; Order; Modesty* in form and style; *Efficiency;* and *Economy.* When accompanied by *Punctuality* . . . a great deal of student writing that meets this criteria—perhaps most of it—should be good enough to receive a good enough grade, a B, in most institutions. (72)

The logical question to pose when reviewing Bloom's list is, Where do students who are deemed "basic" writers fail in their attempts to achieve this broad, "good enough" status in college writing classrooms? Surely among and between these categories, there is room for some variability in assessment? If the definition of "good enough" is supremely *local*, however, there lies the complication in distinguishing between and locating boundaries for "basic" and "standard" first-year writers. For example, applying Bloom's standards for "good enough" to Harvard students in the early twentieth century makes for a difficult enterprise, since modesty was not a valued trait (given the desire for Harvard men to be bold, intellectual leaders), but order was critical. At Yale during this time, however, conformity and conventionality were key, since students were remanded to the Awkward Squad based on their inability to conform to the prescribed style for analyzing literature, as their writing lacked the "decorum" of typical analyses.

Further into the future, Shaughnessy's students were arguably penalized for lacking self-reliance and responsibility in their surface skills, as needing individual, extensive tutoring in grammar and mechanics and lacking the ability to use a prized form of "conventionality"—Standard Written English (especially those who were second-language writers or who were raised in homes using non-standard dialects). Finally, in today's basic writing classrooms—at least in my own—I have seen an ironic twist on the standard value of economy, as many of my students profess being taught in high school that they must "only say what they need" and not "go on and on" in their writing. In these cases, students have been penalized during intake measurements for being too "economic," resulting in a basic writing placement, where they continue to unwittingly limit their means of expression based on a skewed implementation of this value, which was carefully and deliberately formed at the secondary level.

THEORIZING ENDINGS: DECONSTRUCTING *BASIC* AND RECONSTRUCTING PROGRAMS

In order to hypothesize about eliminating the label of *basic* from our first-year writing courses and programs, we must consider the role that such labels play in socializing students into the larger institution. While this book has sought to exemplify this socialization through a close look at Yale's and Harvard's remedial courses in historical context, the larger question of how institutional responses to underprepared student writers govern and sustain such labels transcends the boundaries of elite institutions. Many authors have already uncovered the political and social imperatives at work in the creation of first-year programs, for example Susan Miller's *Textual Carnivals* and Sharon Crowley's *Composition in the University*. I do not seek to replicate that work here. Instead, I want to consider two theoretical perspectives on the present and future state of course delineation in first-year writing programs and examine how these theories, inextricably tied to the ultimate "fate" of composition studies at the university, impact upon any proposal to eliminate basic, remedial, or precollege writing courses.

In *Introducing English: Essays in the Intellectual Work of Composition*, James Slevin argues that "the work of composition always and of necessity begins with interpretation," because at its core, writing instruction involves not only interpreting student texts but also interpreting the difficulty students encounter and display when putting together a piece of academic writing. Slevin categorizes these as difficulties of absence, lack, and difference and asserts, "With respect to the teaching of writing and reading, the response to difficulty interpreted as *lack* is remediation" (14–15). Slevin's discussion of *lack* is critical in an interrogation of basic writing, as it allows for the implementation of "evaluative procedures governed by a teleology of improvement and plotted within a narrative structure of improvement," aligned with "the agency of the work . . . constructed as an accommodation to lack," clearly visible through program design at various types of postsecondary institutions (15). As compared to viewing difficulty as difference, which requires that composition must be work to "*make something* of that difference" (17), difficulty as lack provides institutions with heroic, self-conscious options that keep intact the status quo.

Slevin's chart which follows, sets such responses to lack as "conversion" reactions against "preservation" reactions in this regard:[2]

	Conversion	**Preservation**
Extreme	basic writing	English composition at elite schools
Moderate	English composition at non-elite schools	first-year seminars at elite schools
Modest	required advanced writing	writing across the curriculum (WAC)

Slevin categorizes basic writing as an "extreme" reaction within a conversionist paradigm, whereas standard English composition is more the "moderate" response. The "modest" reaction within conversion strategies is to require an advanced writing course—to situate the "lack" further in the curriculum, thereby embedding its use value within upper-division goals and objectives. Each of these moves seeks to "convert" students to more proficient writers and to guarantee a swift and visible response to the perceived problem of proficiency (or lack thereof). Comparatively, an "extreme" reaction within a preservationist program—one that seeks to maintain standards but without visible markers indicating deficiencies—is to offer standard composition at elite locations—that is, the current situation at Harvard and Yale. Other more moderate approaches involve first-year seminars (see, for example, Dartmouth's and Brown's current first-year curricula). Finally, the most modest approach within preservationist tactics is a writing-across-the-curriculum program, again pushing skill acquisition into the later years of the curriculum.

Whether an institution approaches writing instruction seeking conversion or preservation has to do largely with local values; however, Slevin implies that elite institutions choose preservation—the less-visible, quieter option—over conversion whenever possible. In making this charge, Slevin imbues these institutions with a clear value of *self*-preservation—a desire to uphold the status quo and address writing problems from within rather than categorically and in line with public institutions in response to outside, uniform standards. Slevin's chart, however, fails to include any basic writing curricula at elite institutions and thus fails to reflect the curricular reality, past and present, at schools such as Yale and Harvard, despite the fact that these schools were certainly going through the motions of "preservationist" design throughout the twentieth century.

These comparatives do, in broad strokes, match historical truths about first-year writing at elite institutions and the "extreme" reaction to perceived lack, if we make more fluid the definition of *basic* beyond what Slevin suggests. At Yale, for example, standard composition (training in nonliterature-based expository writing) has been regarded as basic within the institution's curricular structures explicitly through the 1950s; subsequently, the first-year seminar, "Daily Themes," in place at Yale beginning in the late 1950s served as a more "moderate" response to students' writing needs, a more implicit, and less overtly basic course. At Harvard, I would argue that the English A course was created in response to "lacking" elements of refinement present in Harvard student writing and that English C, D, and F were subsequently created to address further perceived deficiencies.

Slevin's positioning of these course types as preservation responses is evident in the archival evidence presented, namely that early versions of both standard and remedial composition at Yale and Harvard were *precisely* designed to preserve the dignity and status of the institution and the quality of its graduates. In contrast, the "extreme" matching response at non-elite schools is, in fact, comparatively positioned as conversion to the values and norms of those schools—to bring students up to the college-level goal, however problematic that may be to define. In both cases, categorizing basic writing or standard composition as extreme allows for the belief that "only improvement, not the construction of lack that is its precondition, can be refused; when refused, improvement gives us misbehaving, or uncivilizable students" (Slevin 15–16).

This belief is illustrated in both Yale and Harvard curricula; in each case, students demonstrating lack were given what each institution construed as open, necessary assistance in order to avoid the impression that the Ivy League might produce "uncivilized" students. Any refusal was on the part of the student—subsequently interpreted as a lack of intellectual seriousness, an affront to the institution's arguably patrician values, or both. At both institutions, the paternalistic view—faculty know best—was in full force, more to maintain the reputation of the respective institutions rather than to raise the expectations for incoming applicants or set a higher bar for admissions.

Slevin's theories of *lack* prefigure later discussions in composition studies regarding the overall future of the discipline, most important, the first-year course that stands at its core. David Smit, in *The End of Composition Studies*, proposes that first-year writing might be disconnected from the field of composition studies and instead taught as an embedded skill within the larger curriculum. Smit further argues that composition studies reposition its graduate programs—specifically those granting the PhD—as being for "research in the discourse practices of particular communities . . . and research in the training of writing teachers for those communities" (198). The "terminal degree . . . for writing teachers" would thus be the MA or a professional certificate. Smit rationalizes this structural shift by noting that the proliferation of adjunct labor and graduate teaching assistants in first-year writing programs has essentially meant the field's concession that a doctoral degree is no longer needed for writing teachers (197). Smit's proposed course would be "Introduction to Writing as a Social Practice" and would involve participation from faculty across the curriculum, with special attention to the discourse and inquiry methods of various disciplines, leading to later advanced courses in "particular knowledge domains" (187–88). His plan is based, in part, on the widely divergent means by which students learn to write, are asked to perform in writing courses, and are taught in writing programs. Smit asserts that his proposal is further built on questioning two assumptions of the field: "that writing is a global or universal activity and that writing, especially at the college level, is in some sense foundational to advanced learning" (10).

Smit's larger project—to question the means by which composition studies controls and disseminates the teaching of writing in the university—and to end its oversight of a "hegemony" of writing instruction (12) is obviously not my mission here. But Smit's larger proposal rests on several smaller assertions that *do* intersect with questions I have raised about definability of basic versus standard composition and the short historical memory of the discipline's standards in deciding that only certain underprepared students are worthy of additional assistance and advocacy in first-year writing. The most critical assertion that Smit makes is this: "Given that the field [of composition studies] is so fragmented, given that many models of the field are that it is 'postmodern,' that knowledge in the field must of necessity be local, historicized, and contingent, reaching any kind of consensus about the teaching of writing will be no easy task (12). Smit argues that composition studies alone thus cannot address all of the competing needs of student writers in the university—that the field continues in its dominance to "foster writing in 'generic' writing courses with no common curriculum or content . . . [even though] what we call writing ability may be a wide range of knowledge and abilities, many of which are highly dependent upon the context in which the writing occurs" (10).

I do not agree with many of Smit's assertions, particularly that the first-year composition course is usually or always content free in its design or that there is not already a developing model for his proposal at work at various institutions, including my own, wherein composition studies faculty can *participate* in the training of teachers and the literacy skill-building of students. But his proposal is notable for not only its embedded observation that our instructional methodologies must be rooted in local histories and contingencies but also that our consideration of student writers must be highly contextualized and mindful of the "range of knowledge and abilities" that students bring to the writing table. Using this platform, Smit envisions what I would call a highly leveled approach to writing instruction at the university, one that eschews ability designations, even if it also minimizes the intellectual contributions that composition studies can bring to this reorganization in the first-year arena.

But every plan, however promising, has a sticking point—and Smit's is the curricular structuring and handling of basic writers. In formulating his plan for widespread university participation in writing instruction, Smit acknowledges that there is "no such thing as instant literacy in any discourse community." Unfortunately, he also asserts that "it certainly takes longer than one or two courses offered as 'remedial' or 'developmental' or 'basic' before students are required to take the usual two-semester introductory writing sequence." Such a claim, in addition to assuming that all universities have the "usual" two semesters of writing also assumes that basic writers, as a group, are *several semesters* away from being able to assimilate into college-level courses. Such a belief fails to recognize the needs—ranging from minimal to extensive—that students present when entering a basic writing classroom and the variety of ways in which proficiency may be determined in any given institutional location. And so, while I agree with Smit's assertion that "part of the solution to the problem of 'basic writing'" must include "holding all those who teach writing at all levels responsible for providing the scaffolding that basic writers need" (188), I disagree that so-called basic writers must be segregated from his cross-curricular writing proposal or others similar to it (for example, the growing WAC and WID university programs nationwide, which Smit acknowledges are integral to his overall plan).

But even if a model such as Smit's has its flaws, we must think about the real possibilities facing the field as enrollments increase, faculty tenure-track lines decrease, budgets constrict and collapse, and universities look to trim, refine, and simplify how first-year writing is delivered and taught. Will basic writers be the first to be sacrificed because they are so easily segregated, even within apparently accommodating and collegewide plans? And if so, are we facing a university of the future that rather than simply labeling students as not ready decides that assisting these students is worth neither the time nor the energy expended? Viewing *all* first-year writing as preparatory in the local context of the *individual college or university*—rather than based on generalized perceptions or standards of preparedness across institutions—does away with the temptation to eliminate access for some or all students who are not ready for the standard course. Rather than viewing such responses along a continuum of urgency—extreme, moderate, or modest proposals, in Slevin's terms—we should eliminate the *basic* label as not only a humane and communally responsible act but a practical and efficient one as well, a means by which we might preserve the diversity and dignity of the first-year students at our schools, by treating these people as intellectual equals in need of the preparation that every student rightfully deserves, but some require in different configurations than others.

CONCLUSION: (DIS)LOCATING BASIC WRITING'S FUTURE

Imagine, if you will, a first-year program at Equitable University that looks like this: A first-year writing curriculum with a menu of course options for incoming (and transfer) students, each with equal course credit, each with a small course capacity (of twelve to fifteen students), and each with a simple, objective name. One course is called "Writing 1." The next is called "Writing 2." The next is called "Writing 3." Each course is regarded publicly—in all marketing for the institution as well as in communication with prospective students and their parents—as college-level, and incoming students are encouraged to choose, through a process of guided self-placement, which course along the sequence best meets their initial needs. No student is called remedial or basic and certainly not precollege (they *have* been admitted, after all, to the university). Students may take Writing 1 and then go through the sequence, or they may take and pass Writing 1 and then skip to Writing 3, if they feel they are ready to move ahead out of sequence. Similarly, students may take Writing 2 or 3 first and then move backwards in the curricular sequence to Writing 1, if they feel they need more assistance. No one is penalized for skipping steps or course levels. Students may repeat courses if they are deemed to need to do the work of the first, second, or third course again (as with any other university course, including foreign languages and mathematics). And no one is labeled as deficient for choosing to make a move in either direction, for any reason.

Of course, this is a broad, utopian vision with no local conditions to complicate it. I have not specified how many students are in this university, from what backgrounds, or with what means they enter (financially, socially, politically) equipped for university life. I have not set down any faculty senate or similar governing body's rules for graduation, credit accrual, regressive credit, or the like. But this is the beauty of the Writing 1-2-3 system and the very point of its design. At the risk of sounding like an infomercial, this is a sequence that *everyone* can use, as opposed to the floating and varied definitions that cause courses to be labeled differentially from college to college, university to university. It is not a standard *curriculum*; it is a *model* that eliminates the stigma, as much as is possible, from different levels of preparedness in first-year writing. It does not purport to say *what the standards should be* or how those standards match some universal definition for the course(s); indeed, by eliminating traditional course titles, no such expectations of alignment exist. Instead, it leaves those local, institutional standards alone, to be employed within the courses' goals and objectives themselves.

Because I have imagined a simple sequence without preconceived notions of student ability, student demographics, or institutional barriers (financial or otherwise, actual or theoretical), I have left wide-open the possibility of adaptation, in addition to the possibility that given the institutional circumstances, there may be more or less than three courses offered; this number is simply a starting position. All I ask is that no part of this sequence—or its students—be called *basic* or mainstream or advanced. It's a simple request, yet one that requires the field of composition studies to let go of its assumptions about remediation, basic writing programs, and basic writing students. It requires that we let our minds travel back to a time before 1970, when students at all manner of colleges and universities and from all possible socioeconomic levels, and all possible cultural backgrounds were actively enrolled in precollege courses. It requires that we *start over* and begin to think forward, even as we fight the temptation to fall back on old habits and tried methods and live blissfully, even ignorantly, in the past. It requires that we remind ourselves of where our students, courses, and larger curricula "live" and how that location is valued by the constituents of the first-year writing program.

It is time, as composition studies is in a new century, to challenge our existing notions of ability testing, curricular designations, and student stratification. Recognizing a more open history of basic writing as we move toward defining the twenty-first-century university allows us to build a stronger defense against and stronger rationale for administrators, legislators, and other higher-education watchdog groups who essentialize first-year writing, including basic or remedial writing and pigeonhole its theoretical and historical roots in a clean and unadulterated box, free from sociopolitical conditions that have heavily influenced the ways in which college writing has been taught. Moreover, our traditional, essentialized view of first-year writing has effectively kept underprepared students at a disadvantage for resources and funding given to other, "regular" students—as these underprepared students represent to legislators an uncomfortable and frustrating result of the always-present weakening of secondary and postsecondary educational outcomes. We need to level the field, and we need to do so now.

One way to address the public's discomfort, in proposed practice, with where basic writing "fits" in the university has been the removal of *all* basic writing curricula from four-year institutions, relegating it to two-year and/or trade colleges—where such students are *expected* to reside (think CUNY, with others surely to follow). Such a displacement denies basic writers the opportunity to enroll in the colleges of their choice until they are "vetted" for that location. Because the evidence I have presented shows that basic writers have been variously defined but uniformly stigmatized over the past eighty years, it is unconscionable to relegate all basic writing to the standard and put-upon location of the community college, as such a separation implies that basic writers are always *exactly the same*—regardless of institutional type or location or local values. It's easy for officials to say basic writing is *always* X, or was never Y, and certainly hasn't been around for more than the last thirty years. We can recall Gail Stygall's charge, voiced in 1994, that we make "the historicity of basic writing 'problem' visible to our colleagues and administrators." Stygall asserts that the need for programs in basic writing is "not temporary, and should not be based on its alleged momentary appearance" ("Resisting Privilege" 339). Stygall argues that by positioning basic writers' needs as part of a fleeting "crisis" in our schools and programs, we allow for the hope that these needs will be eradicated through the passage of time.

By making limited, ahistorical assertions about the places in which basic writers have existed, we ignore the rich models—and powerful lessons—we can take to our classrooms and programs in search of equal institutional status and opportunity for all writing students. In order for research in basic writing to truly contextualize its origins, we must consider *all* sites of instruction when assembling a social history of the basic writer or the student whose writing is outside what is considered standard/acceptable to the institution at hand and the culture in which it operates. Mike Rose has noted that basic writing curricula is "self-contained; that is, [it has] little conceptual or practical connection to the larger writing environment in which students find themselves" ("Remedial" 109). Sharing our varied histories of different models for basic writing courses and recognizing the trajectory of flawed thinking that has pervaded much of this instruction since far before Shaughnessy's work will allow us to see this group of students as ever-changing but ever-present and in need of continual advocacy and curricular invigoration, rather than administrative banishment to a precollege location.

NOTES

WORKS CITED

INDEX

NOTES

Introduction: Relocating Basic Writing

1. This period of 1920 to 1960 has a historical precedent in composition studies research, as it is the same period on which Susan Miller focuses in her investigation of composition course offerings at fifteen private and public universities in "Rereading for the Plot," the second chapter of *Textual Carnivals*.

2. See Laura Gray-Rosendale's monograph *Rethinking Basic Writing: Exploring Identity, Politics, and Community in Interaction* (Mahwah, NJ: Erlbaum, 2000).

1. Locating First-Year Composition

1. See also Johnathon Mauk's essay "Location, Location, Location: The 'Real' (E)states of Being, Writing, and Thinking in Composition," originally published in *College English* 65 (2003): 368–88 and reprinted in Peter Vandenberg, Sue Lum, and Jennifer Clary-Lemon's anthology *Relations, Locations, Positions: Composition Theory for Writing Teachers* (Urbana, IL: NCTE, 2006), 198–225, the latter being the source that I cite in this chapter. Mauk's essay, while arguing for a more theoretical notion of *location* based on a materialist critique of composition programs, still uses a very similar metaphorical starting place in its argument, and thus I owe him due credit here.

2. One might argue that even though alternative-placement initiatives—such as (guided or not) self-placement mechanisms—ostensibly position students as authorities over their own writing instruction, the available guidance (brochures, program material) and faculty involvement necessary and instrumental in most self-placement initiatives still requires that students position themselves as writers along institutionally sanctioned scales or rubrics, thereby eliminating some of their own personal markers of authorship or literacy success. Linda Adler-Kassner and Susanmarie Harrington observe, "Rather than challenging the notion of objective literacy embodied in more traditional placement systems, alternatives like DSP

[directed self-placement] simply ask students to rank themselves against this conception of literacy, rather than having the institution do it for them" (42). As such, the institution—the location—in which the basic course "lives" is still the most critical factor in determining who will enroll in it and for what reasons.

2. Re(Defining) *Basic* in Context

1. For one excellent example of this focus on archival research, see Neal Lerner, "Rejecting the Remedial Brand: The Rise and Fall of the Dartmouth Writing Clinic," *College Composition and Communication* 59.1 (2007): 13–35.

2. The core focus of McAlexander's article is a comparison of Mina Shaughnessy and a contemporary, the overlooked basic writing scholar K. Patricia Cross, who, McAlexander argues, "gives the more accurate answers to questions raised in this debate [over remediation]" in comparison to the widely cited and revered Shaughnessy (29).

3. Lerner further notes that the demise of Dartmouth's Writing Clinic was in part due to its function as "a constant reminder that Dartmouth had a problem [underprepared writers] that just would not go away" (19). Lerner explains that on the basis of recommendations from outside scholars such as Albert Kitzhaber, the writing clinic was dismantled; the argument was made that poor writing was less about *need* than about *effort* in the classroom (25). At Yale, the historical move away from "regular" first-year writing and basic writing initiatives, such as the Awkward Squad, to an emphasis on creative writing-as-composition and the "daily themes" curriculum in the 1960s closely resembles Dartmouth's response to the "no need" rationale, which Lerner argues is driven by "branding words such as *flagship*, *excellence*, and *signature*" (30).

4. The relationship between community-college English faculty and academia's social and economic disregard for remedial writing is obviously worth a historical study of its own, one that this book does not attempt to undertake. A suggested starting point, however, might be Andelora's observation that "during the 1970s and 1980s, [community college faculty] watched the field of rhetoric and composition grow up around them. [As a result], English faculty eventually found themselves in the awkward position of being 'gatekeepers' for standards they did not create and do not control" (7).

3. Before 1960: The Rise of the Boneheads

1. Though the majority of *EJ, CE,* and *CCC* authors were male, several articles located in my study of remedial writing instruction in the 1940s and 1950s were authored by women. Perhaps, this is a nod to the notion of lower-

level writing instruction being "women's work," to paraphrase Sue Ellen Holbrook. Also of note is the structure of these essay publications, which were typically more narrative, structured in whole or part as "stories," in comparison to the more summative, enumerated lists of practices (or advice) found in male-authored essays of the time in these same publications.

2. F. N. Scott, in 1922, goes so far as to blame the shifting *family structure* for the creation of the remedial writer, in that "the breaking up of what may be called the family tradition [led to the loss of] the daily reading of the Scriptures, the earnest admonition of parents, couched frequently in conventional but nevertheless elevated language" as well as the entrance of outside media such as the newspaper, which "has brought into the home smartness, slang, sensation, flippancy, and insincerity" ("English Composition as a Mode of Behavior," 465–66).

4. The "Awkward Squad" and Basic Writing at Yale

1. As one piece of early institutional evidence for this phenomenon, Thomas Masters relates that John Evans, one founder of Wheaton College, Illinois, argued, "It would cost at least a thousand dollars less for each son we may educate in the proposed university than to send him to Yale or Cambridge" (16).

2. It is important to note that at least through World War II, or approximately 1945, Yale's English department was divided into regular faculty and "Faculty of the Freshman Year," whose teaching assignments consisted exclusively of first-year English courses and whose advisees were similarly new students. These faculty were typically but not always assistant professors and lecturers. Such an arrangement, which seems to have been disbanded as Yale's teaching load lessened in midcentury and the institution came to resemble its current Research I shape (2/2 or lower teaching loads, focus on research and scholarship as primary mission), was a precursor to similar experimental arrangements at universities today wherein first-year-studies and freshman-experience courses are offered.

3. For a discussion of the type of military terminology that has been appropriated by American English speakers, including male college students, see Henry Alexander, "Words and the War," *American Speech* 19.4 (1944): 276–80; Bert Jarnagan and Fred Eikel Jr., "North Texas Agricultural College Slang," *American Speech* 23.3–4 (1948): 248–50; and Garland Cannon, "Abbreviations and Acronyms in English Word-Formation," *American Speech* 64.2 (1989): 99–127.

4. Towle was an instructor at this time at Yale who was, in his words, "studying and teaching the Awkward Squad." This may make Towle one of the first self-declared scholars of underprepared students.

5. Further evidence of the financial costs of the individual instruction in the squad may be inferred from a November 15, 1932, letter from Frederick Pottle—apparently the head of a personnel/staffing committee in English—to an instructor, Henry Canby, in the Yale English department. Pottle, responding to Canby's request for additional compensation for an atypical course load for the upcoming semester, says that to grant such a request would require that the department "either omit provision for the Awkward Squad or to drop another instructor."

6. At least five articles on the subject of the Army Specialized Training Program appeared in *College English* between 1942 and 1945: "English in Wartime: A Resolution from the College Section" (Mar. 1942), "English in Wartime: A Symposium by College Teachers" (Feb. 1942), "English for Men in Uniform" (Jan. 1944), "English for Ex-Service Personnel: A Survey Conducted by *College English*" (Jan. 1945), and "Army English Experiences Applicable to Civilian, Postwar English" (Mar. 1945). These articles debated the content, value, and feasibility of the training program. E. A. Walter, at the University of Michigan, notes, incorporating language from the college-section resolution on the subject, in the "English in Wartime" symposium that faculty must "revitalize our decision to teach our students 'clarity, accuracy, and responsibility in thought and communication.' . . . Any progress which we can make toward that goal will help our students not only as active soldiers but as active citizens 'who are honestly and enthusiastically devoted to the society which they create'" (581). Comparatively, Karl Young at Yale University says in the "Wartime" symposium, "The momentary shift in our teaching of our subject ought to be slight, though it will be important. We shall, of course, give a fresh emphasis to democracy and Americans, but probably the shift will not be momentous" (496). R. S. Crane at the University of Chicago voiced similar concerns that "we will not be rushed into making hasty adaptations of our subject to the apparent needs or emotions of the moment" (499). Such a response to the proposed army-based curriculum reflects a sampling of the rough division between embracing patriotic ideals in the form of revised approaches to teaching and to learning in larger public institutions and a resistance to "emotion"-based changes to curriculum among the older and more elite institutions.

7. Wykoff's description of the Purdue Basic Skills/English Army course also included literary appreciation, which, Wykoff noted, was designed to illustrate "the relation of composition to the humanities as represented by literature" so that "those who are themselves skillful in writing can best appreciate the writings of others, then adequate composition teaching could very easily led to a considerable revival of interest in literature

and the humanities" ("Army English Experiences," 338, 342). In other words, one aim in the Purdue course was to inculcate potential students into the English major (literary study), even from this compressed basic English course. Such a goal lays bare the hope that composition will not be divorced from the rest of English studies by virtue of basic composition courses such as these and also previews the function of English composition courses in many departments today as fertile ground for attracting and securing new majors.

5. Beyond English A: Harvard's Basic Writers and "Fatherly" Advice

1. Patricia Donahue notes in *Local Histories*, "The Harvard narrative as a story of origin and imitation has become so deeply entrenched within our discipline as to function as an 'always already' beyond which it can be difficult to go" (222).

2. The rhetoric course was given in the *sophomore* year of instruction, despite the apparent urgency for Harvard men to rectify their writing wrongs, owing to the fact that "no one of the departments which occupy the [first] year [are] willing to give up its time, and each suppor[ts] the other in opposition to change" (Hill, "Answer," 12). Each student was required to write six themes; Hill notes, "The books studied ought to tell on the themes, and they do so tell with faithful students who assimilate what they learn" ("Answer," 13).

3. For a dissenting view, see Donald C. Stewart's 1992 article "Harvard's Influence on English Studies: Perceptions from Three Universities in the Early Twentieth Century," in which he notes, "In 1909–10 Harvard offered nine courses in English composition, all of them essentially skills courses, and not one, with the dubious exception of Barrett Wendell's, taught by anyone who had made a significant theoretical contribution to the field" (457). Stewart contrasts this implicitly minor contribution with work done at other universities, including the University of Michigan, to make the case that Harvard did not make significant *intellectual* or scholarly contributions to the field beyond its first-year curriculum.

4. Though a study of ESL course offerings is not the aim of this book, I believe it is important to note the presence and evolution of the second-language composition course (English for Foreign Students) at Harvard during this time period, for two reasons. First, there is no evidence of such a course being offered at Yale during this era. Second, the ESL course is referenced in several discussions of English C, D, and F at Harvard—significantly whether the other remedial courses were, in fact, chiefly assisting ESL writers (or "foreign" writers, in the language of the time) outside the ESL course itself. In addition, when remedial composition disappears from

the curriculum (circa 1950, with the introduction of the general-education curriculum) so, too, does the English for Foreign Students course. In my opinion, a separate study of second-language programs in the Ivy League during this time period would be a worthy undertaking for another scholar.

5. Many thanks to Nancy Sommers and Karen Heath, who provided me with information about the current Expos program at Harvard and a viewpoint for the goals of Expos 10. Readers should also view Sommers's short film *Shaped by Writing* in order to gain a fuller understanding of the work of the Harvard Expos program and its students in the twenty-first century.

6. Hereafter, I will refer to this group simply as the Committee, for space considerations.

7. In the archived copy of this memo template, which I viewed, *fifteen* is crossed out and in pencil *nineteen* is written above it, apparently a later amendment in reporting. The smaller count is likely the one that was sent to individual faculty.

8. The Committee's work was not limited to simply helping those reported; it also involved predicting need and estimating the number of students who would be reported for further work. For example, I came across a portion of a report in the Harvard archives entitled "Notes on Our Experiment in Selecting Men Likely to Be Reported" (to the Committee) regarding the Class of 1944. Although, unfortunately, the document lacked its second page, the initial available page outlined the Committee's confident calculations showing that of the forty-six men the members believed were "very likely" to be reported, thirty-three received grades in English A of C or D, and one failed. Of these men, seventeen were reported to the Committee. The two other categories of men studied—those who were "less likely" to be reported (no rationale given) and those who "might escape being reported" due to their "moderate errors"—were proportionately much smaller, apparently satisfying the Committee that its members could predict with some accuracy who would need assistance and who would likely not, which somewhat contradicts their assertion to faculty that *all* men could and should benefit from their services and that there is no "danger" in overreporting.

9. Though I feel this is a very appropriate term for the Committee's work, it also deliberately invokes David Bartholomae's famous "Tidy House" essay on basic writing, as there are overlaps between the histories Bartholomae describes in that essay and the social aims of the Committee during this era.

10. White's letter is chiefly concerned with matters of grammatical correctness in student writing, as it includes a long paragraph lamenting that students do not know the difference between *among* and *between, in* and *into,* and other surface-level problems. The letter also evidences White's concern for linguistic refinement in upper-class or elite students in particular, as he further questions aloud, "As each crop of students flocks in . . . I wonder more and more . . . what the preparatory schools are really doing or trying to do."

11. Regrettably, the cartoon is undated; I found it pasted into the "Scrapbook" of the Committee on the Use of English by Students, among letters of interest and support for the program sent by other university chairs and deans, documenting the years between 1917 and 1930. In 1934, the English F course name changed to English C, and the course labeled as English F became a public-speaking course. Thus, given these historical contexts, my best estimate for this cartoon's publication date is during this thirteen-year period. I regret that the date is not more exact.

6. Looking Forward, Looking Back: Locating Basic Writing Today

1. Brian Huot provides a succinct outline of the Spellings Report in the May 2007 issue of *College English.* Huot argues that, among other problems, (1) the report does not address the nontraditional student in its four-year graduation goal, (2) the "rising cost of tuition" and other accommodations go directly to the "business model" promoted by today's economy, which in turn creates higher costs that the "commission laments" in favor of "a stronger social mission and less public funding," (3) "the commission calls for more standardized accountability systems at the same time that it sees a stronger role for faculty governance"; and (4) while "the commission notes the special needs of certain students and of students from certain groups, [it] does not recognize any differences in postsecondary institutions" (522). It is this last point of Huot that is the most applicable to a study of basic writing, as the Spellings report, like other standardized testing models at the secondary level, aims to paint with a broad brush the "typical" college student in measures of accountability and to recognize simultaneously that special-needs students ultimately exist. An application of this policy to basic writing programs would similarly fail to account for not only the disparities in skill and knowledge found within every basic writing classroom (including those incorporating second-language students) but would also likely have little to no regard for the differences between basic writing courses *across* institutions and institutional types.

2. The original chart appears in Slevin, *Introducing English,* 15.

WORKS CITED

Adler-Kassner, Linda, and Susanmarie Harrington. *Basic Writing as a Political Act: Public Conversations about Writing and Literacies*. Cresskill, NJ: Hampton, 2002.

Andelora, Jeffrey. "The Professionalization of Two-Year College English Faculty: 1950–1970." *Teaching English in the Two-Year College* 35 (Sept. 2007): 6–19.

Armstrong, Cherryl. "Reexamining Basic Writing: Lessons from Harvard's Basic Writers." *Journal of Basic Writing* 7 (1988): 68–80.

"Awkward Squad." Def. "The New Buffalo Soldiers: Indian Wars Slang." Dr. John Productions, 2000–6. 10 July 2006 <http://abuffalosoldier.com/slang.htm>.

———. Def. Probert Encyclopedia. 2 July 2006 <http://www.probertencyclopaedia.com/cgi-bin/xphrase.pl?keyword=awkward+squad>.

Bailey, J. O. "Harvard, Yale, Princeton Required English." *South Atlantic Bulletin* 11.4 (1946): 6–8.

Bartholomae, David. "The Study of Error." *College Composition and Communication* 31 (1980): 253–69.

———. "The Tidy House: Basic Writing in the American Curriculum." *Journal of Basic Writing* 12.1 (1993): 4–22.

Berlin, James. *Rhetoric and Reality: Writing Instruction in American Colleges, 1900–1985*. Carbondale: Southern Illinois UP, 1987.

———. *Writing Instruction in Nineteenth Century American Colleges*. Carbondale: Southern Illinois UP, 1984.

Bloom, Lynn Z. "Good Enough Writing: What Is Good Enough Writing, Anyway?" Sullivan and Tinberg 71–91.

Bond, Gilbert L. "A Postwar Program for the Remedial-English Student." *College English* 7 (1946): 466–70.

Brereton, John. *The Origins of Composition Studies in the American College, 1875–1925*. Pittsburgh, PA: U of Pittsburgh P, 1995.

———. "Rethinking Our Archive: A Beginning." *College English* 61 (1999): 574–76.

Briggs, L. B. R. "The Correction of Bad English as a Requirement for Admission to Harvard." Hill, *Twenty Years*, 33–41.

Buck, Norman S. Memo to Stanley T. Williams, Department of English. 22 Dec. 1941. YRG3-A, folder 217, box 21. Yale University Archives.

Cadigan, Robert J. "The Private Secondary School and the College." *College English* 3 (1942): 735–41.

Campbell, JoAnn. "Controlling Voices: The Legacy of English A at Radcliffe College 1883–1917." *College Composition and Communication* 43 (1992): 472–85.

Churchman, Philip H. "Elasticity in Freshman English Courses." *English Journal* 1 (1912): 308–10.

Clark, David Lee. "Classification of Freshmen: The University of Texas." *English Journal* 18 (1929): 330–34.

Cloud, Dudley Hunt. "Remedial English Work." *English Leaflet* 34.344 (1940): 1–9. HUC8939.24.5. Harvard University Archives.

———. Letter to Jerome Greene. 29 June 1939. Committee on the Use of English by Students. UA I 5.168, box 133. Harvard University Archives.

———. Memo to Harvard Faculty. 28 May 1940. Committee on the Use of English by Students Correspondence. UA III 10.61.10. Harvard University Archives.

Coffman, George R. "Correlation between High-School and College English." *English Journal* 11 (1922): 129–39.

"Committee Goes After Men Misusing English on Exams." *Harvard Crimson* 31 May 1951. 31 May 2007 <http://www.thecrimson.com/printer-friendly.aspx?ref=480944>.

Committee on the Use of English by Students. *Annual Reports of the Committee on the Use of English by Students, Harvard University*. 1916–39. UA III 10.61.5. Harvard University Archives.

———. Committee request cards for Harvard faculty. UA III 10.61.10. Harvard University Archives.

———. English D student memo. 24 Feb. 1942. HUC 8938.124, box 763. Harvard University Archives.

———. English F student memo. 18 Dec. 1925. HUC 8938.124, box 763. Harvard University Archives.

———. Instructor memo. Nov. 1925. UA III 10.61.10. Harvard University Archives.

———. Memo to Harvard faculty. 23 Jan. 1918. HUC 8938.124, box 763, Harvard University Archives.

———. Memo to Harvard faculty. 4 Dec. 1942. UA III 10.61.10. Harvard University Archives.

———. "Notes on Our Experiment in Selecting Men Likely to Be Reported." 1944. UA III 10.61.10. Harvard University Archives.

———. Student memo. Dec. 1925. UA III 10.61.10. Harvard University Archives.

Conant, James B. "The Mission of American Universities." *Harvard Alumni Bulletin* 25 (Feb. 1938): 597.

Connors, Robert. *Composition-Rhetoric: Backgrounds, Theory, and Pedagogy*. Pittsburgh, PA: U of Pittsburgh P, 1997.

———. "Overwork and Underpay: Labor and Status of Composition Teachers since 1880." *Rhetoric Review* 9 (1990): 108–26.

"Courses of Instruction." 1917–59. HUC 8500.16, boxes 3–8. Harvard University Archives.

Cox, Martha H., John W. Canario, and James R. Cypher. "Remedial English: A Nation-Wide Survey." *College Composition and Communication* 11 (1960): 237–44.

Crowley, Sharon. *Composition in the University: Historical and Polemical Essays*. Pittsburgh, PA: U of Pittsburgh P, 1998.

DeGenaro, William. "Why Basic Writing Professionals on Regional Campuses Need to Know Their Histories." *Open Words: Access and English Studies* 1 (2006): 54–68.

Delcamp, E. W. "The Value of Post-Graduate Study." *Classical Journal* 23.6 (1928): 448–55.

Donahue, Patricia. "Disciplinary Histories: A Meditation on Beginnings." *Local Histories: Reading the Archives of Composition*. Ed. Donahue and Gretchen Flesher Moon. Pittsburgh, PA: U of Pittsburgh P, 2007. 220–36.

Eble, Kenneth E. "What Happened to the Boneheads?" *News Bulletin of the Rocky Mountain Modern Language Association* 13.4 (1960): 1–3.

Ede, Lisa. *Situating Composition: Composition Studies and the Politics of Location*. Carbondale: Southern Illinois UP, 2004.

"Educational News and Editorial Comment." *School Review* 23.4 (1915): 262–71.

"English F." *Harvard Crimson* 19 Dec. 1923. 31 May 2007 <http://www.thecrimson.com/article.aspx?ref=423400>.

"English for Ex-Service Personnel: A Survey Conducted by *College English*." *College English* 6 (1945): 206–12.

Fountain, Alvin M. "The Problem of the Poorly Prepared Student." *College English* 1 (1940): 309–22.

Fox, Tom. *Defending Access: A Critique of Standards in Higher Education*. Portsmouth, NH: Boynton-Cook, 1999.

Gates, Theodore J. "The First Instruction in Composition." *College English* 3 (1941): 64–69.

Goggin, Maureen Daly. *Authoring a Discipline: Scholarly Journals and the Post–World War II Emergence of Rhetoric and Composition.* Mahwah, NJ: Erlbaum, 2000.

Gordon, Joseph W., and Linda H. Peterson. "Writing at Yale: Past and Present." *ADE Bulletin* 071 (1982): 10–14.

Grey, Lennox, Merritt Y. Hughes, Fred W. Lorch, and George B. Parks. "National Council of Teachers of English College Section." *College English* 3 (1942): 584–86.

Grove, W. Alan. "Freshman Composition: Its Great Middle Class." *College English* 1 (1939): 227–36.

Gunner, Jeanne. "Iconic Discourse: The Troubling Legacy of Mina Shaughnessy." *Journal of Basic Writing* 17.2 (1998): 25–43.

Harris, Joseph. *A Teaching Subject: Composition since 1966.* Upper Saddle River, NJ: Prentice Hall, 1997.

Harvard Lampoon. Cartoon. "Never Mind . . . " Date unknown. Scrapbook, Committee on the Use of English by Students. HUC8938.124, Box 763. Harvard University Archives.

"Has English Zero Seen Its Day? A Symposium." *College Composition and Communication* 8 (1957): 72–95.

Hatfield, W. Wilbur. "English for Men in Uniform." *College English* 5 (1944): 200–206.

Hemingway, S. B. Memo to Provost Charles Seymour. 12 Oct. 1936. YRG 3-A, folder 218, box 21. Yale University Archives.

———. Memo to Provost Charles Seymour. 28 January 1935. YRG 3-A, folder 218, box 21. Yale University Archives.

Hill, Adams Sherman. "An Answer to the Cry for More English." Hill, *Twenty Years*, 6–16.

———, ed. *Twenty Years of School and College English.* Cambridge: Harvard UP, 1896.

Holbrook, Sue Ellen. "Women's Work: The Feminizing of Composition." *Rhetoric Review* 9.2 (1991): 201–29.

Hood, T. L. Memo to Harvard faculty. 25 May 1922. UA III 10.61.10. Harvard University Archives.

Horner, Bruce. "Discoursing Basic Writing." *College Composition and Communication* 47 (1996): 199–221.

Hughes, Helen Sard. "The Prescribed Work in College English: Its Relation to the Secondary Schools." *English Journal* 11 (1922): 199–213.

Huot, Brian. "Consistently Inconsistent: Business and the Spellings Commission Report on Higher Education." *College English* 69 (2007): 512–25.

Jensen, George H. "The Reification of the Basic Writer." *Journal of Basic Writing* 5.1 (1986): 52–64.

Johnson, Paula. "Freshman English in the Ivy League." *Freshman English News* 5.3 (1977): 14–18.

———. "The Politics of 'Back to Basics.'" *ADE Bulletin* 053 (May 1977): 1–4.

Johnson, Paula, and Judith D. Hackman. "The Yale Average: or, After Competence, What?" *College Composition and Communication* 28 (1977): 227–31.

Jolliffe, David. "The Moral Subject in College Composition: A Conceptual Framework and the Case of Harvard, 1865–1900." *College English* 51 (1989): 163–73.

Karabel, Jerome. *The Chosen: The Hidden History of Admission and Exclusion at Harvard, Yale, and Princeton*. New York: Mariner, 2006.

Kitzhaber, Albert R. *Rhetoric in American Colleges, 1850–1900*. Dallas, TX: Southern Methodist UP, 1990.

———. "Syllabus for English 01, Washington State University, 1946–1947." 1 Mar. 2007 <http://comppile.tamucc.edu/archives/kitzhaber.pdf>.

Lerner, Neal. "Rejecting the Remedial Brand: The Rise and Fall of the Dartmouth Writing Clinic." *College Composition and Communication* 59 (2007): 13–35.

Levine, David O. *The American College and the Culture of Aspiration, 1915–1940*. Ithaca, NY: Cornell UP, 1986.

Lu, Min-Zhan. "Conflict and Struggle: The Enemies or Preconditions of Basic Writing?" *College English* 54 (1992): 887–913.

Lunsford, Andrea. "An Historical, Descriptive, and Evaluative Study of Remedial English in American Colleges and Universities." Diss., Ohio State U, 1977.

Marshall, Margaret. *Response to Reform: Composition and the Professionalization of Teaching*. Carbondale: Southern Illinois UP, 2004.

Martz, Louis L. "Annual Report of the Department of English to the President, 1958–1959." Records of Alfred Whitney Griswold. RU-22, folder 722, box 81. Yale University Archives.

Masters, Thomas. *Practicing Writing: The Postwar Discourse of Freshman English*. Pittsburgh, PA: U of Pittsburgh P, 2004.

Mauk, Johnathon. "Location, Location, Location: The 'Real' (E)states of Being, Writing, and Thinking in Composition." *College English* 65 (2003): 368–88. Rpt. in Vandenberg, Lum, and Clary-Lemon 198–225.

McAlexander, Patricia. "Mina Shaughnessy and K. Patricia Cross: The Forgotten Debate over Postsecondary Remediation." *Rhetoric Review* 19.1–2 (2000): 28–41.

McMullen, A. J. Memo to Harvard faculty. 1 April 1932. UA III 10.61.10. Harvard University Archives.

———. Memo to Harvard faculty. 21 October 1936. UA III 10.61.10. Harvard University Archives.

Milhauser, Milton. "Universal English at the University of Bridgeport." *College English* 10 (1949): 340–41.

Miller, H. P. Letter to the Committee on the Use of English by Students. 3 May 1930. Scrapbook of the Committee on the Use of English by Students. UA III 10.61.26. Harvard University Archives.

Miller, Susan. *Textual Carnivals: The Politics of Composition*. Carbondale: Southern Illinois UP, 1991.

Morison, Samuel Eliot. *The Development of Harvard University since the Inauguration of President Eliot 1869–1929*. Cambridge: Harvard UP, 1930.

Mosley, Milka Mustenikova. "The Truth about High School English." Sullivan and Tinberg 58–68.

Mutnick, Deborah. *Writing in an Alien World: Basic Writing and the Struggle for Equality in Higher Education*. Portsmouth, NH: Boynton/Cook, 1995.

Nettleton, George. "Annual Report of the English Department, Yale University, 1929–30." 18 June 1930. RU-24, box 75, folder 758. Yale University Archives.

———. "English at Yale." *Yale Alumni Weekly* 1924: 1061–63. YRG 3-A, series 1, box 21, folder 219. Yale University Archives.

"New Look for English A." *Harvard Crimson* 28 Feb. 1949. 31 May 2007 <http://www.thecrimson.com/printerfriendly.aspx?ref=475037>.

Nibecker, F. H. "Education of Juvenile Delinquents." *Annals of the American Academy of Political and Social Science* 189 (Jan. 1937): 75–84.

Noyes, E. S. "The Program of the Awkward Squad." *English Journal* 18 (1929): 678–80.

"Petition against Military English." English Department Records. UAV 363.418: 1. Harvard University Archives.

Pierson, George W. *Yale College: An Educational History 1871–1921*. New Haven, CT: Yale UP, 1952.

———. *Yale: The University College 1921–1937*. New Haven, CT: Yale UP, 1955.

Pooley, Robert C. "Achieving Continuity in High-School and College English." *College English* 6 (1944): 149–56.

Pottle, Frederick. Letter to Henry Canby. 15 Nov. 1932. YRG 3-A, series 1, box 21. Yale University Archives.

Pound, Louise, Karl Young, P. G. Perrin, Charles Child Walcutt, R. S.

Crane, Louise M. Rosenblatt, Warner G. Rice, George R. Coffman, and Oscar James Campbell. "English in Wartime: A Symposium by College Teachers." *College English* 3 (1942): 495–502.

Rabourn, Susie McD. W. "English Curriculum for Pupils of Low I.Q." *English Journal* 20 (1931): 449–54.

"Report of the Committee on the Use of English by Students." 26 May 1914. Papers of President Abbott Lawrence Lowell. UA I 5.160.2, folder 209. Harvard University Archives.

Rose, Mike. "The Language of Exclusion: Writing Instruction at the University." *College English* 47 (1985): 341–59.

———. "Remedial Writing Courses: A Critique and a Proposal." *College English* 45 (1983): 109–28.

Ross, Edward Alsworth. "The Diseases of Social Structures." *American Journal of Sociology* 24.2 (1918): 139–58.

Russell, David. *Writing in the Academic Disciplines: A Curricular History*. Carbondale: Southern Illinois UP, 1991.

Salvatori, Marolina. *Pedagogy: Disturbing History, 1820–1930*. Pittsburgh, PA: U of Pittsburgh P, 2003.

Scott, Frank N. "English Composition as a Mode of Behavior." *English Journal* 11 (1922): 463–73.

———. To the Committee on the Use of English by Students. 16 Nov. 1919. Scrapbook of the Committee on the Use of English by Students. UA III.10.61.26. Harvard University Archives.

Shaughnessy, Mina. *Errors and Expectations: A Guide for the Teacher of Basic Writing*. New York: Oxford UP, 1977.

———. Introduction. *Journal of Basic Writing* 1.1 (1975): 1–4.

———. Introduction. *Journal of Basic Writing* 1.2 (1975): 1–3.

Sheridan-Rabideau, Mary, and Gordon Brossell. "Finding Basic Writing's Place." *Journal of Basic Writing* 14.1 (1995): 21–26.

Shor, Ira. "Errors and Economics: Inequality Breeds Remediation." *Mainstreaming Basic Writers*. Ed. Gerry McNenny. Mahwah, NJ: Erlbaum, 2001. 29–54.

Slevin, James. *Introducing English: Essays in the Intellectual Work of Composition*. Pittsburgh, PA: U of Pittsburgh P, 2001.

Smit, David. *The End of Composition Studies*. Carbondale: Southern Illinois UP, 2004.

Soliday, Mary. *The Politics of Remediation: Institutional and Student Needs and Higher Education*. Pittsburgh, PA: U of Pittsburgh P, 2003.

Sommers, Nancy. *Shaped by Writing: The Undergraduate Experience*. VHS. Cambridge, MA: Harvard University, 2002.

———. E-mail to the author. 4 Aug. 2006.

Sparling, Edward J. "Improving the Status of the Composition Teacher." *College Composition and Communication* 8 (1957): 67–72.

Stanley, Carrie Ellen. "This Game of Writing: A Study in Remedial English." *College English* 4 (1943): 423–28.

Stewart, Donald C. "Harvard's Influence on English Studies: Perceptions from Three Universities in the Early Twentieth Century." *College Composition and Communication* 43 (1992): 455–71.

"Students Apt to Be Temperamental, Curious, or Amused When Sent to English F, Says McMullen—Few Harvard Graduates." *Harvard Crimson* 1 Mar. 1932. 31 May 2007 <http://www.thecrimson.com/printerfriendly.aspx?ref=181766>.

Stygall, Gail. "Politics and Proof in Basic Writing." *Journal of Basic Writing* 7.2 (1988): 28–41.

———. "Resisting Privilege: Basic Writing and Foucault's Author Function." *College Composition and Communication* 45 (1994): 320–41.

Sullivan, Patrick. "An Essential Question: What Is 'College-Level' Writing?" Sullivan and Tinberg 1–30.

Sullivan, Patrick, and Howard Tinberg, eds. *What Is "College-Level" Writing?* Urbana, IL: NCTE, 2006.

Synott, Marcia G. "The Admission and Assimilation of Minority Students at Harvard, Yale, and Princeton, 1900–1970." *History of Education Quarterly* 19.3 (1979): 285–304.

———. "The Changing 'Harvard Student': Ethnicity, Race and Gender." *Yards and Gates: Gender in Harvard and Radcliffe's History.* Ed. Laurel Thatcher Ulrich. New York: Palgrave, 2004. 195–211.

Tatlock, John Strong Perry. "English." *Harvard Professors Write about Their Own Departments.* 1929. Harvard University. HUC 8929.23A. Harvard University Archives.

Towle, Carroll S. "The Awkward Squad at Yale." *English Journal* 18 (1929): 672–77.

Troyka, Lynn Quitman. "Defining Basic Writing in Context." *A Sourcebook for Basic Writing Teachers.* Ed. Theresa Enos. New York: Random, 1987. 2–14.

Vandenberg, Peter, Sue Hum, and Jennifer Clay-Lemon. "Critical Introduction." Vandenberg, Hum, and Clay-Lemon 1–20.

———, eds. *Relations, Locations, Positions: Composition Theory for Writing Teachers.* Urbana, IL: NCTE, 2067.

Varnum, Robin. "The History of Composition: Reclaiming Our Lost Generations." *JAC* 12.1 (1992). 1 Aug. 2007 <http://www.jacweb.org/Archived_volumes/Text_articles/V12_I1_Varnum.htm>.

White, Henry Adelbert. Letter to the Committee on the Use of English by Students. 6 Nov. 1922. Scrapbook of the Committee on the Use of English by Students. UA III 10.61.26. Harvard University Archives.

Whitney, Norman J. “Ability Grouping at Syracuse.” *English Journal* 13 (1924): 482–89.

Williams, Joseph. Letter. *ADE* 46 (1975). 1 June 2007 <http://www.mla.org/ade/bulletin/N046/046999.htm>.

Williams, Mentor, Ben Euwema, Arthur H. Nethercot, Gerald Sanders, Fred W. Lorch, E. A. Walter, George B. Parks, Ernest C. Hassold, B. E. Boothe, James H. Hanford, and Norman Nelson. “English in Wartime: A Resolution from the College Section.” *College English* 3 (1942): 578–84.

Williams, Stanley T. Memo to Provost Edward Furniss. 22 Jan. 1942. YRG 3-A, folder 217, box 21. Yale University Archives.

Wozniak, John. *English Composition in Eastern Colleges, 1850–1940*. Washington, DC: UP of America, 1978.

Wright, H. Bunker. “What Freshman Composition Cannot Do.” *College English* 7 (1945): 98–101.

Wykoff, George S. “Army English Experiences Applicable to Civilian, Postwar English.” *College English* 6 (1945): 338–42.

———. “An Open Letter to the Educational Experts on Teaching Composition.” *College English* 1 (1939): 140–46.

———. “Results and Cost of Eleven Semesters of SubFreshman English Instruction.” *College Composition and Communication* 12 (1961): 217–23.

———. “Teaching Composition as a Career.” *College English* 1 (1940): 426–37.

“Yale College Courses for the Freshman Year, 1945.” Y65.1 1945. Yale University Archives.

Yale Freshman Committee. “Syllabus for Basic English: Army Specialized Tutoring Program.” 10 May 1943. YRG 3-A, folder 216, box 21. Yale University Archives.

“Yale Undergraduate Courses of Study. 1919–1951.” YJA65 A11. Yale University Archives.

Yancey, Kathleen Blake. *Delivering College Composition: The Fifth Canon*. Portsmouth, NH: Boynton/Cook, 2006.

Yancey, Kathleen Blake, and Brian M. Morrison. “Coming to Terms: Vocabulary as a Means of Defining First-year Composition.” Sullivan and Tinberg 267–81.

INDEX

CCCC STUDIES IN WRITING & RHETORIC

Edited by Joseph Harris, Duke University

The aim of the CCCC Studies in Writing & Rhetoric (SWR) series is to influence how writing gets taught at the college level. The methods of studies vary from the critical to historical to linguistic to ethnographic, and their authors draw on work in various fields that inform composition—including rhetoric, communication, education, discourse analysis, psychology, cultural studies, and literature. Their focuses are similarly diverse—ranging from individual writers and teachers, to classrooms and communities and curricula, to analyses of the social, political, and material contexts of writing and its teaching. Still, all SWR volumes try in some way to inform the practice of writing students, teachers, or administrators. Their approach is synthetic, their style concise and pointed. Complete manuscripts run from 40,000 to 50,000 words, or about 150 to 200 pages. Authors should imagine their work in the hands of writing teachers as well as on library shelves.

SWR was one of the first scholarly book series to focus on the teaching of writing. It was established in 1980 by the Conference on College Composition and Communication (CCCC) to promote research in the emerging field of writing studies. Since its inception, the series has been copublished by Southern Illinois University Press. As the field has grown, the research sponsored by SWR has continued to articulate the commitment of CCCC to supporting the work of writing teachers as reflective practitioners and intellectuals. For a list of previous SWR books, see the SWR link on the SIU Press website at www.siu.edu/~siupress.

We are eager to identify influential work in writing and rhetoric as it emerges. We thus ask authors to send us project proposals that clearly situate their work in the field and show how they aim to redirect our ongoing conversations about writing and its teaching. Proposals should include an overview of the project, a brief annotated table of contents, and a sample chapter. They should not exceed 10,000 words.

To submit a proposal or to contact the series editor, please go to http://uwp.aas.duke.edu/cccc/swr/.

OTHER BOOKS IN THE CCCC STUDIES IN WRITING & RHETORIC SERIES

African American Literacies Unleashed: Vernacular English and the Composition Classroom
Arnetha F. Ball and Ted Lardner

Rhetoric and Reality: Writing Instruction in American Colleges, 1900–1985
James A. Berlin

Writing Instruction in Nineteenth-Century American Colleges
James A. Berlin

Something Old, Something New: College Writing Teachers and Classroom Change
Wendy Bishop

The Variables of Composition: Process and Product in a Business Setting
Glenn J. Broadhead and Richard C. Freed

Audience Expectations and Teacher Demands
Robert Brooke and John Hendricks

Archives of Instruction: Nineteenth-Century Rhetorics, Readers, and Composition Books in the United States
Jean Ferguson Carr, Stephen L. Carr, and Lucille M. Schultz

Rehearsing New Roles: How College Students Develop as Writers
Lee Ann Carroll

Dialogue, Dialectic, and Conversation: A Social Perspective on the Function of Writing
Gregory Clark

Toward a Grammar of Passages
Richard M. Coe

A Communion of Friendship: Literacy, Spiritual Practice, and Women in Recovery
Beth Daniell

Rural Literacies
Kim Donehower, Charlotte Hogg, and Eileen E. Schell

Embodied Literacies: Imageword and a Poetics of Teaching
Kristie S. Fleckenstein

Writing with Authority: Students' Roles as Writers in Cross-National Perspective
David Foster

Writing Groups: History, Theory, and Implications
Anne Ruggles Gere

Sexuality and the Politics of Ethos in the Writing Classroom
Zan Meyer Gonçalves

Teaching/Writing in Thirdspaces: The Studio Approach
Rhonda C. Grego and Nancy S. Thompson

Computers & Composing: How the New Technologies Are Changing Writing
Jeanne W. Halpern and Sarah Liggett

Teaching Writing as a Second Language
Alice S. Horning

Revisionary Rhetoric, Feminist Pedagogy, and Multigenre Texts
Julie Jung

Women Writing the Academy: Audience, Authority, and Transformation
Gesa E. Kirsch

Invention as a Social Act
Karen Burke LeFevre

A New Perspective on Cohesion in Expository Paragraphs
Robin Bell Markels

Response to Reform: Composition and the Professionalization of Teaching
Margaret J. Marshall

Gender Influences: Reading Student Texts
Donnalee Rubin

The Young Composers: Composition's Beginnings in Nineteenth-Century Schools
Lucille M. Schultz

Multiliteracies for a Digital Age
Stuart A. Selber

Technology and Literacy in the Twenty-First Century: The Importance of Paying Attention
Cynthia L. Selfe

Language Diversity in the Classroom: From Intention to Practice
Edited by Geneva Smitherman and Victor Villanueva

Whistlin' and Crowin' Women of Appalachia: Literacy Practices since College
Katherine Kelleher Sohn

Across Property Lines: Textual Ownership in Writing Groups
Candace Spigelman

Personally Speaking: Experience as Evidence in Academic Discourse
Candace Spigelman

Self-Development and College Writing
Nick Tingle

Mutuality in the Rhetoric and Composition Classroom
David L. Wallace and Helen Rothschild Ewald

A Taste for Language: Literacy, Class, and English Studies
James Ray Watkins

Evaluating College Writing Programs
Stephen P. Witte and Lester Faigley

Minor Re/Visions: Asian American Literacy Narratives as a Rhetoric of Citizenship
Morris Young

Kelly Ritter is an associate professor of English at the University of North Carolina–Greensboro, where she directs the first-year composition program and teaches graduate and undergraduate courses in composition studies. Her essays and articles have appeared in *College Composition and Communication*, *College English*, *Composition Studies*, *JAC*, *Pedagogy*, *Rhetoric Review*, and *WPA: Writing Program Administration*. She is also the coeditor (with Stephanie Vanderslice) of *Can It Really Be Taught? Resisting Lore in Creative Writing Pedagogy*.